D1789360

REVIEWS OF UNITED KINGDOM

STATISTICAL SOURCES

Volume V

General Sources of Statistics

Reviews of United Kingdom Statistical Sources

Editor W. F. Maunder

REVIEWS OF UNITED KINGDOM STATISTICAL SOURCES
Edited by W. F. Maunder
Professor of Economic and Social Statistics
University of Exeter

VOLUME V

GENERAL SOURCES OF STATISTICS

by

G. F. LOCK

Research Division, House of Commons Library

Published for
The Royal Statistical Society and
the Social Science Research Council
by

HEINEMANN EDUCATIONAL BOOKS
LONDON

Heinemann Educational Books Ltd.

LONDON   EDINBURGH   MELBOURNE   AUCKLAND   TORONTO
JOHANNESBURG   NAIROBI   IBADAN   LUSAKA
HONG KONG   SINGAPORE   KUALA LUMPUR   NEW DELHI

ISBN 0 435 82543 7
© Royal Statistical Society
and Social Science Research Council 1976
First Published 1976

For bibliographical purposes this volume should be cited as:
Lock, G. F., *General Sources of Statistics*, Heinemann Educational Books on behalf of The Royal Statistical
Society and the Social Science Research Council, 1976

Published by Heinemann Educational Books Ltd.
48 Charles Street, London W1X 8AH

Printed in Great Britain by
Cox & Wyman Ltd.,
London, Fakenham and Reading

FOREWORD

The Sources and Nature of the Statistics of the United Kingdom produced under the auspices of the Royal Statistical Society and edited by Maurice Kendall, filled a notable gap on the library shelves when it made its appearance in the early post-war years. Through a series of critical reviews by many of the foremost national experts, it constituted a valuable contemporary guide to statisticians working in many fields as well as a benchmark to which historians of the development of Statistics in this country are likely to return again and again. The Social Science Research Council and the Society were both delighted when Professor Maunder came forward with the proposal that a revised version should be produced, indicating as well his willingness to take on the onerous task of editor. The two bodies were more than happy to act as co-sponsors of the project and to help in its planning through a joint steering committee. The result, we are confident, will be adjudged a worthy successor to the previous volumes by the very much larger 'statistics public' that has come into being in the intervening years.

Dr C. S. Smith

Secretary
Social Science Research Council

February 1976

E. M. L. Beale

Honorary Secretary
Royal Statistical Society

February 1976

MEMBERSHIP OF THE JOINT STEERING COMMITTEE

(February 1976)

Chairman: Professor Sir Roy Allen

Representing the Royal Statistical Society:

    Dr W. R. Buckland

    Miss S. V. Cunliffe

    Dr S. Rosenbaum

Representing the Social Science Research Council:

    Mr A. Noble

    Mr T. S. Pilling

    Dr W. Taylor

Secretary: Mr D. E. Allen

Introduction

This volume, the fifth in the series, is to be sharply distinguished from the normal run of its companion reviews providing, as it does, an overview of almost the whole field of economic and social statistical sources. Its inclusion in the series was prompted by several reasons.

First and foremost, there are many users of statistical data whose requirements do not call for an intensive study of the topic in which they are interested. Next, there are those who are concerning themselves with the subject of sources for the first time, and clearly, for them, a bird's eye view of the forest is the best beginning. It is hoped, for example, that the present review may be a particularly suitable reference manual for social science students either in first year university courses or in adult education classes. Finally, and somewhat paradoxically, this review serves the purpose of dealing with a wide range of published sources which receive scant attention in the rest of the series; these are the secondary publication sources (like the *Annual Abstract of Statistics* and the *Monthly Digest of Statistics* to take obvious examples) in which most of the information comes from other primary sources. Indeed, as the author pointed out in early discussions, it is a review of general sources and not a general review of sources. For these objectives, it may be thought particularly interesting that the review is the contribution of a research statistician operating under 'front-line' conditions in a key library which, no doubt, provides ample exposure to the day-to-day needs of at least some of the classes of users discussed above.

Although the subject matter of the review ranges over the whole field of economic and social statistical sources, it may be pertinent to point out that it does not thereby constitute a definitive frame for the whole series, as might be supposed. Doubtless, this would have been a very laudable and logical objective but it would have involved a germanic thoroughness quite alien to the spirit of the policy behind the series for which the touchstone is one of pragmatic evolution. A hint on the shape of things to come is given by a quick check on some 25 topics at present in the pipeline at one stage or another, against the Subject Index to the present review: only about a half of the titles could be associated with an entry in the present work. On the other hand, it may be taken as an ambition that virtually every topic mentioned in the present work will eventually form the subject – or part of the subject – of a full review.

The arrangement of this review is, not unnaturally, a law unto itself and it cannot conform to the standard pattern for the series. However, in so far as the material permits, an attempt has been made to retain something of what it is hoped is becoming the familiar arrangement. The review is in three main sections of which the first provides a general background discussion taking in topics such as the relations between the compilers and the users of statistical material, the intricacies of parliamentary and other official publication categories, and the very practical problem of how to get what you want from your librarian. Chapter 2 consists of a summary account of each of the chief published general sources of statistics. Discontinued serial publications are grouped separately from those still currently appearing and an indication is given on how to link or supplement one source with another. In the third and final chapter the author puts forward some ideas on how the whole class of sources reviewed might be developed and improved in the future in order better to meet the needs of users. This last section is, of course, very much a personal view but it is based upon his intimate experience in the House of Commons Library in trying to meet the requirements of users with particularly taxing demands.

In this review there is no Quick Reference List of individual series (which obviously would be outside the scope of its intentions) but its place is taken by a list of the publications dealt with in Chapter 2 which contains the main essential bibliographical information. Easy reference back to Chapter 2 is provided by the serial numbering in the form [QRL Serial Number]. As usual, there is a general bibliography of works discussing wider aspects and in this case text references are made in the form [B Serial Number].

Comments made above have attempted to emphasize the distinctive nature of this review and, by implication, to apprise the reader who has not had occasion to consult any of the other volumes that it should not be regarded as exemplifying the normal treatment. However, it may be stressed that the standing invitation for 'feed-back' from the readership none the less applies. Users will be rendering an invaluable service to their fellows if they will send me a note of specific instances where they have not found the help expected in consulting a review.

As Editor, I again express my very grateful thanks to all the members and the Secretary of the Joint Steering Committee of the Royal Statistical Society and the Social Science Research Council. Grateful appreciation should also be expressed to Paul Richardson and Philippa Stratton of Heinemann Educational Books for all their most co-operative help. The Subject Index of entries for the review was compiled by Marian Reed to whom both the author and I are indebted for her careful patience. It should also be recorded that Mrs Gill Skinner, of the Social Studies Data Processing Unit at the University of Exeter, continues to supervise the computer programmes, which both provide print-outs of individual review indexes and incorporate them into the cumulative index which is held on magnetic tape. The latter is available for keyword search on individual application to me at the Department of Economics, University of Exeter.

University of Exeter   W. F. Maunder
February 1976

Contents

List of Abbreviations used in the
Text and Bibliography

CIPFA   Chartered Institute of Public Finance and Accountancy
COI   Central Office of Information
CSO   Central Statistical Office
DES   Department of Education and Science
DOE   Department of the Environment
DHSS   Department of Health and Social Security
EEC   European Economic Community
GDP   Gross Domestic Product
GLC   Greater London Council
GSS   Government Statistical Service
HMSO   Her Majesty's Stationery Office
IMTA   Institute of Municipal Treasurers and Accountants
ILO   International Labour Office
JRSS   Journal of the Royal Statistical Society, Series A
LCES   London and Cambridge Economic Service
NEDO   National Economic Development Office
OECD   Organization for Economic Co-operation and Development
OEEC   Organization for European Economic Co-operation
PEP   Political and Economic Planning
PIB   Prices and Incomes Board (National Board for Prices and Incomes)
RSS   Royal Statistical Society
SDD   Scottish Development Department
SMMT   Society of Motor Manufacturers and Traders

Author's Introduction

The other reviews in this series deal with the statistics of specific subjects; this review surveys general statistical publications which contain figures on a variety of subjects, and which are much consulted by the non-specialist user of statistics. The other reviews deal in detail with the tables on their subjects in general publications and there is no attempt in this one to compete with these commentaries; a full account of the contents of all general publications would in any case be very lengthy. This review provides a brief commentary on the publications it covers, outlining their scope and giving background information about them intended to assist users. As a prologue to this material on general statistical sources, I have dealt briefly with the following two groups of subjects, of which some knowledge can be helpful to the user of UK official statistical publications:

1. The history and organization of official statistics in the UK.
2. Categories of official publications, indexes and catalogues; explanatory matter; and difficulties in the tracing and location of statistical publications generally.

There are also some summary remarks on non-official statistical publications.

The scope of the review is the United Kingdom and the separate countries thereof, but not publications on individual regions, nor publications on the Channel Islands and the Isle of Man (of which there is in any case a dearth).

References are given as follows:

[QRL 1] means item 1 in the Quick Reference List at the end of the review.
[B 1] means item 1 in the General Bibliography.
‡ means that additional matter is included in the Addenda.

Table I is the table at the end which analyses the subject content of certain sources. Sources included in this table have the sign† after their titles at the beginning of each note in Chapter 2. The sign†† after the names of certain statistical publications is used to refer the reader to the Central Statistical Office's *List of Principal Statistical Series and Publications* [B 15] for bibliographical details. These publications are mentioned only as examples in this review, and it would have increased the length of an already long bibliography too much to have cited every publication mentioned. The less well-known publications, however, which are not in the CSO's *List* are included in the bibliography.

Acknowledgements

I am grateful to the Editor, Professor W. F. Maunder, for advice and encouragement during the lengthy gestation period of the review, and to members of his Steering Committee. I am also very grateful to the following who are among those who have read parts or the whole of the draft: Mrs M. Chapman, Mrs S. Hastings, Mr C. G. Lewis, Mrs M. Nissel, Mr J. Palmer, Miss J. B. Tanfield, Mr A. R. Thatcher, Mr E. C. Thompson and Mr G. D. N. Worswick. They provided corrections on many points, but responsibility for the remaining errors (of which I should be glad to be notified) is of course mine. They are also not responsible for the opinions expressed, which are my own and not those of the House of Commons Library. I should also like to thank Mrs P. Pritchard for coping cheerfully with the typing of an ever-lengthening draft and Mrs D. Meynell for help with reading the proofs.

Reference Date of the Sources Reviewed

The original reference date of this review was 30 November 1972; some of the sources it covers have been affected by changes since then, and I have incorporated into the text the effect of some of the changes made up to mid-1974. The subject-analysis of sources in Table I has not however been revised as this would have involved virtually a repetition of the previous work, but the information on prices of publications in the Quick Reference List has been revised. I have added brief notes on three new general sources that have been published since November 1972 and these appear in Sections 2.2.38–2.2.40. I have also added some items to the bibliography, including the titles of some statistical series mentioned as examples in the text, which were not originally included. In neither case are the contents of these two 'postscripts' sorted into the categories used in the main part of the review, but these deviations from its scheme seemed admissible in the interests of updating.

Addenda

The following notes written at proof-stage in October 1975 record some of the recent changes affecting the subject matter of the review.

Section 1.1 The history and organization of official statistics in the U.K.
The White Papers on government lending, mentioned as survivors from the early 1960s, have now been dropped. (For details of the successive titles see [1] *Additional References* below.) One table is now carried over into the *Financial Statement and Budget Report*††.

The *Public Expenditure White Papers*†† (perversely covered in blue from the 1973 edition) now have ten year runs of figures making longer-run comparisons possible. Some of the improvements in the publication have been instigated by successive reports of the General Sub-Committee of the Expenditure Committee of the House of Commons. Only the first *White Paper* in the series (Cmnd. 4234) included projections of public sector receipts for comparison with the projections of expenditure. Detailed expenditure figures for a long period on a uniform price basis are to be found (for selected years) in *The Developing System of Public Expenditure Management and Control* by Sir Samuel Goldman [2] – *Additional References* below.

Statistical News [B24] p. 24.28, announced that the *Handbook of Statistics* [B148] of the Department of the Environment is due to be revived; it had not however appeared at the time of writing.

The effect of UK membership of the EEC on government statistics is described in a paper of 1973 by Sir Claus Moser and I. Beesley – [3] and [4] *Additional References*. The paper shows that all parts of GSS work are affected, but particularly regional, industrial and transport statistics.

Section 1.2 Relations between compilers and users
Statistical News [B24], p. 29.7, has an article on the National and Local Government Statistical Liaison Committee which is mentioned in this section.

Section 1.3.1 Official publications – categories
Supplementary Statistics Relating to Crime [B168] have now been incorporated into *Criminal Statistics for England and Wales*,†† as from the 1974 issue. Annual reports of public corporations continue to cause difficulty. One recent development is that some of the reports of the Area Electricity Boards no longer include the reports of the Consultative Councils, although the Electricity Act, 1957 apparently requires their inclusion.

Section 1.10 General statistical publications on cities and areas
An addition may be mentioned to the list of regional compilations of statistics – *North West Region – Economic and Social Trends* [5] – *Additional References* below.

Section 2 General sources of statistics
This note does not attempt systematically to update the whole text of the section, but mentions changes in some of the publications covered.

Section 2.2.1 Abstract of Regional Statistics [QRL1]

A new feature of the 1974 issue is a section of 'regional profiles' containing a selection of key indicators on each region with comparisons for the U.K. as a whole.

Section 2.2.6 Department of Employment Gazette [QRL6]

A change was made in 1974 in the publication arrangements for the *New Earnings Survey*††; whereas in previous years the *Gazette* carried several articles on the topic, in 1974 it included only one article, containing the main results. Other tables came out in a series of six booklets for which a binder is available, and a composite book will also appear containing all the published results.

Employment figures for individual localities will not be available for 1974, because of the uncertain basis of the information on local government employment, in the wake of local government reorganization in England and Wales. (*Gazette*, June 1975, p. 522).

Section 2.2.8 Digest of Welsh Statistics [QRL8]

The quarterly periodical mentioned at the end of the Section – *Progress in Wales – Quarterly Summaries of Economic Developments* [B160] changed its title with the issue for the first quarter 1975 to *Welsh Economic Bulletin – A Quarterly Summary of Welsh Facts and Figures*.

The *Annual Report on Wales* [QRL20] was discontinued after the issue covering 1973.

Section 2.2.9 Economic Trends [QRL9]

As mentioned in the review, changes were planned in the arrangement of *Economic Trends*, and these came into effect with the issue for March 1975. The publication was greatly expanded, and now has more tables and charts on key economic indicators. These are preceded by a 'stop – press' section on the latest figures and followed by the articles, which have the same scope as before, and by brief notes on developments in economic statistics. The price rose as a result of these changes, and this rise might be thought to strengthen the case for a 'cheap and expendable monthly', mentioned in Section 3.3. An annual supplement is planned containing very long runs of the main economic series.

A further collection of articles was reprinted in 1975 in the series *New Contributions to Economic Statistics* – [6] *Additional References* below.

Section 2.2.13 Northern Ireland Economic Report [QRL13]

This was discontinued with the 1973 issue, and replaced by *Social and Economic Trends in Northern Ireland* [7] – *Additional References*. The first issue, for 1975, consists of a page and a half of text and about 60 simple graphs and charts. The price – £2.50 – seems excessive, and it is doubtful if the publication is an improvement on the series it supersedes.

Section 2.2.17 Social Trends [QRL17]

The 1974 issue devoted its social commentary to differences between the sexes, included two new sections on children and the elderly, and introduced as a new feature a 'Calendar of Social Events'. The latter summarizes changes in the law and other events which are significant in the social field.

Section 2.2.32 British Political Facts [QRL32]

A new edition was published in 1975 – see [8] *Additional References*, below.

Section 2.2.33 Facts in Focus [QRL33]
A second edition appeared in 1974, broadly along the same lines as the first, but with more emphasis on social and environmental statistics, more regional analysis, and a selection of statistics on EEC member countries, Japan, USA and the USSR. The new edition has 176 tables and 37 charts on the UK, and 20 tables and 3 charts on the EEC.

Section 2.2.38 The General Household Survey [QRL38]
A second Report has now appeared, on 1972: [9] – *Additional References*. This resembles the first Report, but has less commentary and methodological matter. New topics include housing costs, household theft, medicine taking and smoking.

Section 2.2.39 Local Government Trends [QRL39]
The 1974 issue has now been published on much the same lines as the first issue, but with additional material on regionalism and local government finance; [10] – *Additional References*.

Section 3.1 Needs and Desirable Improvements – Government publications generally.
In the list of economic planning documents, the 1973 NEDO paper should also have been mentioned – [11] – *Additional References*.
A footnote mentions that there was no *Quinquennial Review of the National Insurance Scheme* for 1964-8. It seems that there is to be none for 1969-73 either, so the system of regular comprehensive reports to Parliament on the subject has apparently broken down.

Section 3.3 Needs and Desirable Improvements – General sources
The text mentions the difficulties formerly encountered over official figures on the combined impact of means tests – the so-called 'poverty trap'. The 1975 issue of *Social Trends* [QRL 17] has some material on this subject.
Finally, a list is given in *Additional References* of some new descriptive publications on statistical sources.

Additional References

[1] Title varies:- *Government Expenditure Below the Line*
    1961/2–1964/65
    Loans from the Consolidated Fund
    1965/66–1967/68
    Loans from the National Loans Fund
    1968/69–1974/75
    Annual. Command papers.

[2] Goldman, Sir Samuel. *The Developing System of Public Expenditure Management and Control*, HMSO, 1973.

[3] Moser, Sir Claus and Beesley, I.B., United Kingdom official statistics and the European Communities, 1973. *JRSS*, **136**, 539.

[4] Moser, Sir Claus and Beesley, I.B., United Kingdom official statistics and the European Communities, 1973. *Statistical News*, **22**, 1. (A shortened version of item [3].)

[5] *North West Region: Economic and Social Trends.* North West Economic Planning Council, Manchester, 1973 and 1974 eds.

[6] *New Contributions to Economic Statistics,* 7th Series, Dec. 1971 to Dec. 1973. Studies in official statistics no. 24.

[7] *Social and Economic Trends in Northern Ireland* Annual. 1975 – HMSO, Belfast.

[8] Butler, D. and Sloman, A. *British Political Facts 1900–1975,* Macmillan, 1975.

[9] *The General Household Survey 1972*, HMSO, 1975.

[10] *Local Government Trends, 1974*, CIPFA, 1975.

[11] *Industrial Review to 1977*, NEDO, 1973.

[12] Critchley, R. A. *UK Advertising Statistics: A Review of the Principal Source and Figures. The Advertising Association*, 1975.

[13] Comfort, A. F. and Loveless, C. *Guide to Government Data*, Macmillan 1974. This book is primarily a guide to unpublished material on the social sciences in the libraries of government departments in London but it was originally intended to include brief surveys of published material. Such surveys were in the event done for only a few departments: the notes on education and health statistics may be found useful, as may those on statistics produced by the Departments of Employment and the Environment. Some departments are however not covered by the book in respect of either their published or their unpublished material.

[14] *Government Research and Development: a Guide to Sources of Information.* HMSO, 1974.

[15] A series of sixteen separate text-books produced or to be produced by the Open University on statistical sources. The first fourteen "units" are concerned at least partly with UK statistics and cover respectively:- politics; vital statistics; population; housing; education; crime and suicide; production; consumption; investment; labour; inflation; income distribution; transport and communication; trade and balance of payments. Various authors. Course D291. The Open University Press, 1975–

[16] National Institute of Economic and Social Research. *The United Kingdom Economy, 1975.* Commission of the European Communities, Studies – Economic and Finance Series 1975 no. 9. Available through HMSO. A general survey in seven chapters, with twenty-four statistical tables and a good bibliography.

1 UK Statistical Sources—General Background

1.1 The history and organization of official statistics in the UK

A knowledge of how official statistics are organized in this country will help users of statistical publications, and some historical background is given here which may interest users of historical statistics. In most developed countries, there is a central organization responsible for the collection of statistics on all the subjects with which the government is concerned, and for all official statistical publications. This pattern has not been adopted in this country; on most subjects each government department collects and publishes its own statistics, with the Central Statistical Office (CSO) exercising a co-ordinating role and bringing out certain mostly general publications on its own account.[1]

The setting-up of such a central department was recommended as long ago as 1881 [B 82] by a Committee on Official Statistics which found that official statistical publications, 'taken collectively, as the official statistical statement of the condition of the people, present confusion amounting to chaos. It is indeed a huge and forbidding mass of figures without order, harmony, or proportion.'[2] No such department was set up as a result of their recommendations, and the matter was raised again with a Committee on Official Statistics appointed in 1920 [B 89]. A petition had been presented to the government by the Royal Statistical Society (RSS), with many signatures

[1] On the issue of a centralized versus a decentralized system see Carter and Roy [B 29] Chapter XII, Treasury [B 68], pp. 13–15, Moser [B 51], p. 2, Moser [B 53], pp. 4–5 and Pyatt [B 56], pp. 40 and 43.

[2] The Treasury Minute appointing the Committee stated that information that MPs required was often available in official publications but 'so imbedded in masses of detail that it is no wonder Members shrink from the labour of extracting it for themselves.' Some aspects of this situation are still familiar.

including those of leading economists. Other submissions were made by the RSS in 1909 and 1943; see [B 57] and [B 79]. In a complacent report, the Committee, consisting entirely of officials, rejected the proposal for a CSO, which would 'both extend the functions of government and alter the constitutional balance of governmental machinery ... The existence of a CSO would give rise to constitutional and other difficulties', and 'it would do little if anything to remove the conditions which at present limit the production of national statistics'. The Committee recognized that the First World War had done much to stimulate the interest of departments in statistics ([B 89], p. 4), but it needed the stimulus of the Second World War to bring about the foundation of the CSO.

The state of British official statistics between the wars was described in 1946 by the Clapham Committee as follows ([B 86], p. 5):

> If before the war we had been asked to appraise official arrangements for collecting material relevant to economic and social questions, we should have found it hard to deliver a very favourable verdict. In the nineteenth century British official statistics led the world. In the twentieth century, however, their comparative performance has not always been as good. Both on the demographic and on the economic side, it would have been easy to point to serious deficiencies in the state of our official statistics.

As a former Permanent Secretary to the Treasury wrote: 'Departmental statistics did not provide material on many matters on which the state had to lay down policy; nor could one rely on cohesion or consistency between the different sets of figures collected by departments' (Bridges

[B 46], p. 91). Two political scientists commented: 'This system, or lack of system, had been criticized for many years, and a consultative committee was set up in 1920 for co-ordination between Departments. But effective co-operation was enforced only by experience in the war of 1939' (Mackenzie and Grove [B50], p. 99; see also Treasury [B 68], pp. 15–18 and Mosley [B 54], pp. 66–8).

The foundation of the CSO in 1941 is described in the works just cited, so the account will not be repeated here. The next milestone was the 1944 White Paper on *Employment Policy* (Cmd. 6527), which set out the scope of the statistics needed for the operation of the post-war employment policy (quoted in Campion [B 48], p. 3). Two years later, the statistician class was created as a separate specialist class within the Civil Service. The 1947 Statistics of Trade Act extended the statutory powers under which departments could operate, and was the first Act to give general powers for the collection of official economic statistics. Progress continued for the next nine years in the implementation of the 1944 programme, notably in the fields of the national income and balance of payments. In 1956, the then Chancellor of the Exchequer, Mr Macmillan, made his often-quoted comparison of British economic statistics with last year's Bradshaw (railway time-table) [B 71]. This was followed after some months by a statement on a programme for improvements [B 72]. One notable such improvement was the publication, in early 1957, of the first official quarterly estimates of the gross domestic product (GDP). At about this time Political and Economic Planning (PEP) concluded, notwithstanding Mr Macmillan's remarks, that 'it is now widely held that British economic statistics are equal to the best in the world' ([B 108], p. 17), a view echoed by Professor Allen ([B 102], p. 361).

Three years later, the *Report of the Committee on the Working of the Monetary System* (Cmnd. 827) critically reviewed the state of financial statistics, and commented on the reluctance of the Bank of England to publish the statistics at its disposal. As a result of this Report, *Financial Statistics*†† was started and also the *Bank of England Quarterly Bulletin*††; developments were described in an article in September 1962 [B 64]. Also in that year came the White Paper on *Incomes Policy: the Next Step* (Cmnd. 1626) which called for the regular publication of information relevant to wage negotiations. (See below in the note on *Statistics on Incomes, Prices, Employment and Production* [QRL 26], 2.2.26.)

At the end of 1966 the Report of the Estimates Committee on Government Statistical Services was published [B 69]—a substantial report with a mass of oral and written evidence, the repercussions of which are still continuing. Also in that year, Mr E. F. Jackson was 'invited to advise what improvements in official statistics are needed in connection with the implementation of the National Plan, with particular reference to its regional aspects' [B 74]; no report was however published [B 76]. Some new statistical publications and plans for others were surveyed in the 1969 White Paper *Information and the Public Interest* [B 78].*

The recent period is well covered in the following articles and will therefore be dealt with rapidly here: Moser [B 51, 52, 53], Allen [B 44] and Berman [B 45]. (Berman has a useful chronology covering the period 1940–70.) In 1969 the Business Statistics Office was established to take over the functions of the former Board of Trade Census Office, and in the following year the Office of Population Censuses and Surveys was formed as a result of a merger between the General Register Office and the Government Social Survey.

In the past few years more emphasis has been placed on social statistics, which had previously been relatively neglected. The Heyworth Committee on Social Studies reported in 1965 that much remained to be done in respect of the provision, co-ordination and publication of social statistics [B 116], p. 43. The same point was made

---

* Specialized fields are also sometimes surveyed in this way: see for example the 1965 Housing White Paper [B 77].

by the Estimates Committee which called for a 'development of social statistics in the next decade comparable to that which has taken place in economic statistics in the last' ([B 69], p. xxxiv). Another feature of the last few years has been the larger co-ordinating role played by the CSO.

There has long been a link between policy considerations and government statistical work as reflected in publications. In the post-war period, the emphasis was at first on the macro-economic series needed for the management of the economy; then, with the greater reliance on monetary policy, on monetary and financial statistics; and next, on statistics that might influence wage settlements. 'Policy pressures to improve the statistical basis for social policy are more recent' (Moser, [B 53]), but as mentioned above more resources are now being devoted to social statistics. The Estimates Committee ([B 69], p. xvii), quoting from a memorandum by the present writer, referred to 'growth determined ... by the pressure of separate demands', and recommended that the CSO should co-ordinate the development and revision of government statistical publications. On the work of the Government Statistical Service (GSS) generally (as distinct from just its publications), the CSO has now assumed a co-ordinating role. As its Director wrote: 'The CSO will ... work out overall programmes and priorities, and will move towards a comprehensive phased programme of current statistical work up to five years or more ahead' (Moser [B 51]).

So far the fields discussed have been fields of expansion, and there have of course been other such fields: for example, statistics of education, housing, health and overseas aid. Offsetting these have been fields of contraction: one was annual reports of ministries and public corporations, and these are discussed in more detail later (see 1.8); another was publications on overseas countries, with the dropping of the *Overseas Economic Surveys* on separate countries [B 124], the *Digest of Colonial Statistics* [B 121], the *Annual Report on Colonial Territories* [B 119] and the *Statistical*

Abstract for the British Commonwealth and the Sterling Area [B 128]; a third was general economic papers which combined figures and text, mostly produced by the Treasury. The early 1960s were the ‡peak period for these; papers were started at that time on government lending and on public investment, and full annual surveys of both the UK economy and the Scottish economy continued. Within a few years all except the first had been dropped (see below, 2.2.22 and 2.2.23), and in exchange the *Public Expenditure White Papers*††★ were started.

Another factor in the development of UK statistics is the changing relationship between the central government and country authorities in Scotland, Northern Ireland and Wales, as regards both publications and statistical practices. On publications, two contrary tendencies are apparent —towards fragmentation (resulting from the increased delegation mentioned below in 2.1) and towards aggregation. On the one hand, for example, there are now three reports on roads where there used to be one (and the Welsh one is so slight that few national totals could be constructed from the three separate reports); and many of the figures in the *Annual Report of the Department of Health and Social Security*†† (DHSS) refer only to England, as do some in the *Annual Report of the Department of Education and Science* ‡(DES) [B 132] and in the *Handbook of Statistics* [B 148], now discontinued, of the Department of the Environment (DOE). All of these once covered England and Wales. On the other hand, there has been an increase in the number of joint publications designed to bridge the gap resulting from administrative devolution—UK statistics on edu-

* Their primary purpose is naturally to assist in the control of ‡public expenditure and they are only secondarily a statistical source. In the latter capacity they present a number of difficulties: with constant changes of classification; with the annual change of pricing basis which hinders the construction of long runs; and with the impossibility of straightforward comparison between forecast and outcome—a feature shared by government planning documents for the economy as a whole. An attempt has recently been made to assist the user by the publication of a methodological handbook.

cation and agriculture (the latter of long standing), and Great Britain statistics on highways, housing and health (summary tables for GB at the start of *Health and Personal Social Services for England*††). One of the functions of the CSO is to bring together, in several of its general publications discussed later in this review, figures for individual countries and to aggregate them into totals for the United Kingdom or Great Britain.

As long ago as 1877 the Treasury referred to 'the evils of differences in form in compiling statistics in the same subject for England, Scotland and Ireland, and the want of harmony in the headings, classifications, dates and other points where statistics ... ought to be made capable of inter-comparison' ([B 82], p. iv). People using the population census reports eighty-five years later might have wondered how much the situation had changed. The Estimates Committee commented: 'Reports (on the Census) vary in form as between the three authorities and statistics are frequently not fully comparable, making it impossible to produce cumulative totals for the United Kingdom'. [B 69]. A great improvement was however made in the 1966 Census reports, with the production of many tables for Great Britain as a whole and some for the United Kingdom. The problem of comparability within the UK is however not wholly a matter of the Census—there are for example difficulties with some local government statistics—and in some fields it cannot be solved, because of differences in legal, educational and other systems.

1.2   Relations between compilers of statistics and users outside government

More attention has been paid to this subject in recent years than formerly. In some fields there were always arrangements for consultation—for example the advisory committee on the Census of Production. (There were advisory panels with a similar function for the 1971 population census on various subjects with members drawn from inside and outside government; see Bishop [B 61], p. 31.

Such bodies also exist for the indexes of retail prices and the New Earnings Survey and there are informal liaison panels on other topics.) In pre-CSO days, one possible channel was closed, as the Permanent Consultative Committee (see 1.5.1) was specifically debarred from receiving representations from non-official statisticians or organizations ([B 89], p. 13). The Interdepartmental Committee on Social and Economic Research was set up in 1947 partly to promote co-operation between universities and government departments, but its main concern was with academic research (see 1.5.1, footnote).* When Carter and Roy came to report in 1953 they found that 'at present there exists no adequate means by which they [users outside the civil service] can encourage the statistical machine to adapt itself to their ... requirements' ([B 29], pp. 13–15), and they recommended 'the establishment of closer and more widespread contact between official providers and unofficial users of economic statistics'. Twelve years later, the Estimates Committee took evidence from some business users of statistics, and laid great emphasis in their report on the needs of users. (For a further view of official statistics from a business standpoint, see Zinkin and Booer [B 59].)

Professor Moser referred to the matter both at the RSS meeting following the Estimates Committee's report ([B 61], pp. 66–7) and in the first issue of *Statistical News* [B 51] when he said that the CSO would 'pursue any constructive proposals designed to improve the links between the producers and the consumers of official statistics'. The starting of *Statistical News* itself was a notable step forward in communication in one direction. Some of the CSO's proposals were set out in a further paper by Moser in 1971 ([B 53], pp. 22–3).

* A previous body, with a wider remit, lasted only five years—the Committee on Civil Research, which was 'charged with the duty of giving connected forethought from a central standpoint to the development of economic, scientific and statistical research in relation to civil policy and administration.' (Treasury minute of 13 June 1925, Cmd. 2440, quoted in Willson [B 58], p. 322.) The Committee was not a success.

These discussions of the subject were concerned primarily with businessmen, and secondarily with applied economists, but as Carter and Roy pointed out, there are other important categories of users—journalists, historians and even politicians. 'If there is no informed group, fully supplied with facts, which can be thinking freely about future changes in policy, the conduct of affairs will tend to become inflexible. In particular, political controversy will tend to become sterile if Her Majesty's Opposition is rendered incapable of planning intelligent alternative policies' ([B 29], p. 131). (See also Lock in *Statistical News* [B 49], p. 12.9.) To these groups may be added statisticians in local government who were few when Carter and Roy wrote but are now an important and growing class of user. A committee was set up in 1970 specifically to improve the links between local government statisticians and the GSS—the National and Local Government Statistical Liaison ‡Committee ([B 24], p. 13.30).

The steps taken by the CSO to improve the outward flow of information are described in the two papers by Moser cited above, and Berman's paper also refers to the matter, saying that the CSO has made a 'conscious effort to improve the presentation and hence the usefulness of official economic statistics'. On the feedback from the user to the compiler, progress has perhaps been less marked. Some official statisticians actively seek the views of users on their products. When the Perks Committee was sitting, copies of *Criminal Statistics for England and Wales*†† contained reply-paid postcards for users to return; the editor of the *Scottish Abstract* [QRL 15] also used this procedure, and other compilers have sent out questionnaires. Prefaces of official publications sometimes invite comments, and one now usually gains the impression that views are welcome, which was not invariably so in the past. Market research has been conducted on some publications including, among the series dealt with in this review, *Trade and Industry* [QRL 18] and the *Department of Employment Gazette* [QRL 6]. It

would be interesting to know if a correspondence section has ever been considered for *Statistical News*, in which users would be encouraged to discuss official statistics.*

Since October 1970 there have been five statistics users' conferences—respectively on business, social, industrial, labour and EEC statistics; attendance is however necessarily restricted [B 92, 95, 96]. There is also a Standing Committee of Statistics Users, the functions of which relate mainly to sponsoring the users' conferences, though a sub-committee has done some work on the population census. In 1972 the Organization of Professional Users of Statistics was founded, bringing together representatives of five organizations, and having as one of its functions liaison with government in the statistical field. There is however nothing similar for users not belonging to these organizations, and it may be doubted if the ideal institutional framework has yet been found for relations between non-government users and compilers.

I.3 Official Publications

I.3.I *Categories*

Most of the widely used statistical publications in this country are produced by the government, so it is advisable for the user to have some understanding of categories of official publications to use the statistical ones to the best advantage. The subject is complicated, and the account given here concentrates on the aspects which are important to those interested in statistics.

The two most important categories of official publications are parliamentary and non-parliamentary papers. Until the early 1920s life was fairly simple, as most statistical publications of any importance were parliamentary papers—House

---

* There was a vigorous exchange, but too lengthy for a correspondence column, between Professor Townsend and DHSS statisticians on statistics of poverty in the *Political Quarterly*, 1972, pp. 103 and 232.

of Commons or Command Papers.* Over the past fifty years, statistical publications have been transferred to the non-parliamentary category so that now very few are parliamentary papers. The consequences of the transfer for the user include:

1. He needs to consult different indexes.
2. He may find that libraries shelve the non-parliamentary part of a series of publications in a different place from the parliamentary part.
3. He may find that libraries are more selective in their intake of non-parliamentary than of parliamentary papers (on the erroneous assumption that the latter are necessarily more important), and that they therefore do not stock the non-parliamentary part of a series.

The transfer of statistical publications took place largely during two periods—in the early 1920s and from the early 1950s onwards. The format of parliamentary papers was reduced in 1921 and there was an economy drive in government printing. (One factor in the arrangements was that MPs were originally deprived of free copies of papers transferred to the non-parliamentary list.) Examples of papers transferred at this date are the *Annual Statement of Trade*†† and the *Census of Population*†† The motive for the later transfers was no doubt to secure the greater clarity and better layout which the larger size of page makes possible. (Parliamentary papers are restricted to one size only—royal octavo.) The 1950s and 1960s saw the transfer of the recently started series on the balance of payments, the

national income and statistics of fuel and power; the *Annual Abstract* [QRL 2] had been non-parliamentary from the first post-war issue. This process has continued, and an associated development has been the hiving-off of the statistical part of a parliamentary publication into a separate publication in the larger non-parliamentary format—for example *Statistics of Education*††, *Health and Personal Social Services Statistics for England*††, *Inland Revenue Statistics*†† and the separate *Surveys of Personal Incomes*††, all of which originally formed part of departmental reports. The chief regular statistical papers remaining in the parliamentary category, apart from financial papers, are criminal and civil judicial statistics and other papers on various subjects presented by the Home Office. There are however other papers of statistical interest in the parliamentary category—reports of Royal Commissions and of some Committees of Enquiry (but their evidence, if published, is usually non-parliamentary), reports and evidence of Select Committees, and reports of the Monopolies Commission and of the Prices and Incomes Board (PIB), wound up in 1971.

'Non-parliamentary publications' are the publications of Her Majesty's Stationery Office (HMSO) other than parliamentary papers; almost all government statistical publications are now in this category.

Besides parliamentary and non-parliamentary papers, three other categories of official and semi-official statistical publications may be distinguished:

1. Priced publications issued by government departments direct and not through HMSO.
2. Free departmental publications.
3. Publications of organizations other than government departments, which may similarly be free or priced.

These categories may include publications of which earlier issues were parliamentary or non-parliamentary papers; such transfers are not recorded in any one source as these categories are in general excluded from indexes published by

---

* It is difficult to be brief and accurate about the difference between these two types, but the following may give a rough idea. House of Commons papers include papers which are presented to Parliament by Departments because of a statutory obligation. Command papers are presented by Ministers otherwise than under a statute: they should be 'documents relating to matters likely to be the subject of early legislation, or which may be regarded as otherwise essential to Members of Parliament as a whole to enable them to discharge their responsibilities'. (Treasury letter 38/21). On House of Lords papers, see 1.3.3.2, *infra*.

HMSO. All these three categories are therefore more difficult to trace than normal parliamentary or non-parliamentary publications. Examples of papers in these categories are:

1. Priced departmental publications:

   Output and Utilisation of Farm Produce††— formerly part of *Agricultural Statistics, UK*†† (non-parliamentary).

   Some issues of *Housing Survey Reports* [B 152] and of *Statistics for Town and Country Planning* [B 167] (others are non-parliamentary).

   Publications by the Ministry of Agriculture, Fisheries and Food on Farm Rents, Agricultural Land Prices and the Structure of the Agricultural Labour Force.

   Monthly statistics available on subscription from Customs and Excise on spirits, wine and betting duties.

2. Free departmental publications:

   The *Annual Report of the Civil Service Commission* [B 140] (once a parliamentary paper, subsequently a non-parliamentary paper).

   ‡ *Supplementary Statistics Relating to Crime* [B 168].

   Digest of Statistics Analysing Certificates of Incapacity for Work [B 122].

   A Welsh Budget 1968–9 [B 171].

   A Scottish Budget 1967–8 [B 165]. (A similar paper for 1952–3 was parliamentary as were papers that appeared intermittently between 1891 and 1935.)

3. Publications of other bodies:

   There are two important batches of transferred publications:

   (a) those formerly published by HMSO for the Commonwealth Economic Committee but now published by the Commonwealth Secretariat on its own account.

   (b) Annual reports of the nationalized industries.

There were earlier instances of a drift from the parliamentary category to own-account publication: for example, the reports of the Bank of England, Cable and Wireless and London Transport. .

Since 1972 all the nationalized industries have removed their reports from the parliamentary ‡category, with the consequence that HMSO has ceased to handle some of the reports it formerly published and users have to obtain them from the separate corporations. As examples of the situation at the beginning of 1974, HMSO handles the reports of seven of the area electricity boards in England and Wales but not those of the other five; it handles the report of the Electricity Supply Industry Training Board, but not those of other Training Boards; and it handles the report of the Independent Broadcasting Authority, but not that of the BBC.

Apart from their annual reports, some public corporations issue important statistical publications directly: for example, the *Statistical Yearbook* of the Central Electricity Generating Board [B 137] and the *Annual Statistics for the Iron and Steel Industry* [B 154], published by the British Steel Corporation.

It can be the case that official figures are published only in a private enterprise publication; one example is figures of the yield of motor vehicle taxation, analysed by type of vehicle. For the last ten years these have not appeared in any official publication, but only in *The Motor Industry of Great Britain* [B 156], published annually by the Society of Motor Manufacturers and Traders (SMMT). In a slightly different category, because the vehicle revenue figures were once published in a government publication, are figures bought from a government body and then published by the body buying them. Examples are ward details from the population census for its area published by the Greater London Council, and detailed trade

* From 1933 until 1962 London Transport published its own report and has done so again from 1970 on the transfer of the undertaking to the control of the GLC. The Report was a parliamentary paper from 1963 to 1969.

statistics purchased from the Customs and Excise by trade associations and published in their journals, ahead of their appearance in the *Annual Statement of Trade*††.

Another non-departmental publishing body that may be mentioned is the National Economic Development Office (NEDO). It publishes some of its own publications itself (some free and some priced), and some are published by HMSO. With some series, for example statistics on electronics and the motor industry, some issues are published by HMSO and some by NEDO.

1.3.2   *Indexes*
It will be apparent from the examples given above that some official publications can be difficult to trace. The indexes available to assist the user will now be briefly described.

Parliamentary Papers. A sessional index is compiled for use in conjunction with sets of papers bound up and paginated according to the official scheme. The index starts with numerical lists of Bills, House of Commons Papers and Command Papers with volume and page references,* but the most useful part of the index is the alphabetical subject index which follows. This is provided with ample cross-references, and recent sessional indexes conclude with an index of chairmen of committees and other authors of reports. These sessional indexes are consolidated into decennial and fifty-year indexes, the use of which can save a great deal of time if somebody wants references over a long period.

HMSO Annual Catalogues. These cover all parliamentary and non-parliamentary publications except statutory instruments. The statistical user will be mainly concerned with Part II of the catalogue—the classified list, arranged by government department, the list of periodicals, and the title index at the back. Part II has since 1949

covered both parliamentary and non-parliamentary publications, and the index contains enough 'key words' to enable the user generally to trace papers easily. The indexes are cumulated quinquennially (and have been since 1936–40), and the pagination of the catalogue runs consecutively for five years so that they may be bound together. There is a supplement on the publications of international organizations, and the catalogues are kept up to date by monthly and daily lists.

HMSO Sectional Lists. About forty separate lists are published, each dealing with the publications of a department or group of departments. The lists are concerned mostly with non-parliamentary publications (except statutory instruments), but a few lists also contain a selection of parliamentary papers. When the set of lists is complete, it will comprise a complete catalogue of current non-parliamentary publications in print; no such consolidated list for all departments together has appeared since 1920. The lists are brought up to date from time to time, and they are issued free of charge. Among those likely to be of most interest to users of statistics are:

No. 3   Departments of Trade, Industry, Energy, and Prices and Consumer Protection. This gives details, *inter alia*, of the reports on the *Censuses of Production*†† and *Distribution*†† and of the *Business Monitors*††.

No. 28   Periodicals and Subscription Rates—lists statistical periodicals, including the *Business Monitors*†† which are also in list No. 3.

No. 32   HM Treasury and Allied Departments—includes the Central Statistical Office (CSO).

No. 50   Miscellaneous List—includes Customs and Excise (*Annual Statements of Trade*††), those publications of the National Economic Development Office which are published by HMSO, the Registrar General for Scotland

* A fresh numerical sequence is started each session for House of Commons papers and bills (separately). The numbers of Command papers run on from session to session, the current 'Cmnd.' series having started in 1956/7. The previous 'Cmd.' series covered the period from 1919 onwards.

and some reports of the Government Social Survey, which are also in list No. 56.

No. 56 Office of Population Censuses and Surveys.

Publications of departments, public corporations, etc. There are no comprehensive indexes of these. Some items are mentioned in *Statistical News* [B 24] or the *British National Bibliography*. NEDO publishes a six-monthly list of its publications (with a supplement after three months), and the Commonwealth Secretariat brings out an occasional list. Users must hope that this category will be fully dealt with in the CSO's forthcoming *Guide to Current Official Statistics* (see 1.5.1).

1.3.3 *Special classes of official publications*

1.3.3.1 *Publications of the Government of Northern Ireland.* The government of Northern Ireland issues its own publications through HMSO, Belfast, and these are not covered by any of the indexes to government publications mentioned above. Northern Ireland has its own series of House of Commons/Assembly Papers and Command Papers; the former are numbered in one continuous series, unlike the papers of the UK parliament which start a new series each session. There are also non-parliamentary publications, and most statistical papers are in this category. Examples are the *Digest of Statistics* [QRL 7], *Northern Ireland Population Census*††, *Family Expenditure Survey*††, *Northern Ireland Education Statistics*†† and *Digest of Housing Statistics for Northern Ireland*††. Consolidated indexes cover the periods 1921–37 and 1938–47, and subsequent years have annual indexes. There is a monthly list which brings the annual lists up to date. A selection of important publications of the government of Northern Ireland is included in the bibliography of the *Ulster Year Book* [QRL 19]. Official statistics of Northern Ireland were described by A. T. Park in *Statistical News* [B 55]. (Since the prorogation of the Stormont Parliament, House of Commons papers have appeared as non-parliamentary publications.)

1.3.3.2 *House of Lords Papers.* Some papers are presented only to the House of Lords and not to the House of Commons as well. Just occasionally one of these is of statistical interest, for example one published on violent crimes in cities in 1951, and one on statistics of dogs and road accidents caused by them, published in 1959. The House has its own Select Committees, the Reports of which appear as House of Lords papers (but not also as House of Commons papers); examples of recent subjects are sport and leisure and sex discrimination. No consolidated indexes have been produced since that for 1871–84/5, and papers for recent years are best found in the Stationery Office Annual Catalogues.

1.3.3.3 *Hansard.* Much useful statistical information is given in answers to parliamentary questions, both written and oral. This is true of both Houses, but the number of questions is much larger in the House of Commons. Hansard appears in daily and weekly form, and in bound volumes each covering about a fortnight. Written answers are printed at the end of the report of proceedings for the day, and in the bound volumes all written answers for the period are collected together at the end of the volume. Indexes appear weekly, for the bound volumes and for complete sessions. Unfortunately the indexes are not wholly satisfactory and it can be a matter of chance whether a user finds what he is looking for or not. (One drawback is that similar items are not always indexed under the same subject heading.) *Trade and Industry* [QRL 18] reprints, and indexes, selected parliamentary answers within the ambit of its departments; *Housing Statistics* [B 123] also used to reprint some answers, but its successor—*Housing and Construction Statistics*††—has not followed suit. Anybody wishing to make substantial use of statistical material in *Hansard* has little alternative to compiling his own index for the material that interests him.

1.4 Non-official Publications

Although most of the important statistical publications on the UK are official, there are several fields in which non-official publications are important. The distinction between official and non-official is in any case not hard and fast, but 'official' is used in this review to mean the publications of HMSO, government departments, the nationalized industries and some international organizations. This definition is not however comprehensive since it would exclude documents published by, say, NEDO or Economic Planning Councils on their own account. This section outlines some of the main types of non-official publication.

Some general publications are dealt with later in the review in detail, so will not be further commented on here [QRL 4, 12, 25, 27–30, 32, 35–7 and 39]. To a large extent these form useful complements to official publications, in that they carry out functions not performed by the latter. One field in which non-official statistics are very important is local government, where the publications of the Chartered Institute of Public Finance and Accountancy (CIPFA)★ are indispensable. Some of its publications are produced jointly with the Society of County Treasurers, and some on its own; the Society also produces some publications independently. Between them the two organizations cover *inter alia* statistics of education, police, libraries, local finance, highways, water and housing. Most of the figures relate to individual authorities, but national averages are also generally included, as well as averages for different classes of authorities. Sometimes there is both an official publication and an Institute publication in the same field, but where this is so, they treat different aspects; for example, the Institute publishes *Education Statistics* [B 144], and the DES also includes some statistics for individual authorities in its *Statistics of Education*††. The subject of

★ Formerly the Institute of Municipal Treasurers and Accountants (IMTA). The Institute has a Scottish branch with independent publications.

housing rents of individual local authorities is left entirely to the Institute south of the border, whereas in Scotland the corresponding figures are produced by the Scottish Development Department (SDD) in a Command Paper. The latest Institute venture is *Local Government Trends* [QRL 39] which is described briefly in Section 2.2.39.

Another important category of non-official publications is those produced by trade bodies for the industries they represent—for example, the Society of Motor Manufacturers and Traders (SMMT), the British Insurance Association and the Timber Trades Federation. Other trades have statistical organizations solely engaged in the compilation of statistics, such as the World Bureau of Non-Ferrous Metals Statistics, the Wool Industry Bureau of Statistics, and the Audit Bureau of Circulations (for the press). Yet other bodies publish statistics on their own operations as a by-product to their main function—for example the Stock Exchange, the Horserace Betting Levy Board and the University Central Council on Admissions. Another category of publications is those of bodies concerned to advance a particular object such as those of the Churches' Committee on Gambling, the Royal Society for the Prevention of Accidents and the British Road Federation. A few publications are produced as normal publishing ventures like *The Times 1000*, *Moodies Investment Handbooks* [B 155] and F. Craig's admirable series of compilations of election statistics [B 111]. Finally—and these categories are not intended to be systematic or exhaustive—there are non-official publications not exactly fitting into any of the groups suggested, such as *Facts and Figures about the Church of England* [B 145] and the *Occasional Bulletin* of the Nationwide Building Society [B 158].

Taken as a whole, there is thus a considerable body of statistical material, mostly of a specialized nature, that is compiled and published outside the GSS. Not very much of it is included in official general publications; some examples of material so included are the FT-Actuaries indexes of security prices, figures on the operations of the Stock Exchange and the results of surveys of borrowing conducted by the Building Societies Association.

1.5   Guides to Statistical Sources

1.5.1   *Official guides.* As mentioned earlier, the 1881 Committee on Official Statistics recommended the setting-up of a small central statistical department, and among the tasks such a department was to perform was 'the compilation of an annual index to the returns presented to Parliament' ([B 82], p. xxiii). Nothing was done, and the 1921 Committee returned to the subject, saying: 'We have been impressed in the course of our deliberations by the fact that there exists nothing in the nature of a comprehensive index to the numerous volumes of a statistical character, or containing statistics, which are published by the various government departments. We think that such an index would be of great value to all persons who have occasion to use official statistics, and we believe that if it existed it would do much to dispel many . . . misapprehensions as to official statistics' ([B 89], p. 15). This time, some action followed: a Permanent Consultative Committee on Official Statistics was set up, and the first *Guide to Current Official Statistics* was published in 1923 [B 7]. The Consultative Committee did not meet after 1936 ([B 68], p. 14), but the *Guide* carried on until the outbreak of the Second World War. All issues were priced at one shilling and the last issue ran to over 400 pages.

Nothing similar has appeared in the post-war period, but in 1965 the CSO published a thirty-six-page list of economic, financial and regional statistics [B 16]. A new edition, enlarged to cover demographic and social statistics, appeared in 1972 —*List of Principal Statistical Series* [B 15], and a further edition in 1974. Amendments are printed quarterly in successive issues of *Statistical News* [B 24].

However the Estimates Committee in 1966 had recommended the publication of a comprehensive guide, considering that there was all the more need compared with before the war. They recommended 'that there should be made available to the public a comprehensive guide to official and semi-official statistics which is revised periodically and which refers the user to explanatory matter and commentaries'. The government reply to this recommendation said that the problems involved would be re-examined, the work of preparing an adequate guide would be considerable, and that a mere catalogue like the pre-war *Guide* would not be sufficient [B 70]. In February 1970, an assistant director of the CSO said that 'it would be a tremendous undertaking to cover all government statistics', and that the staff for this task was lacking ([B 91], p. 45). The staffing problems have now apparently been overcome, and the preface of the 1972 *List of Principal Statistical Series* ([B 15], p. v) stated that 'the CSO has started work on producing a guide with much the same degree of detail as the pre-war *Guide to Current Official Statistics*', but that 'this cannot be ready for a considerable time'. It is now thought that the new *Guide* might be published in mid-1976. A proposal for a computerized index to the contents of statistical sources is under investigation at the University of Loughborough, but is so far only at the stage of a feasibility study (see [B 114]).

For the moment therefore, until the appearance of a comprehensive guide the user must have recourse to guides on specific subjects, and these are listed in the bibliography. (Some of these were published a long time ago but are still useful as long as one bears their age in mind. I have not included some old lists of statistical series on subjects where the amount published has changed out of all recognition since they were compiled, for example the lists of financial statistical series included in the evidence of the Radcliffe Committee in 1959.) At one time these guides usually appeared under the auspices of the Interdepartmental Committee on Social and Economic

Research,* but recently they have appeared in other series.

For new publications, as opposed to a guide to *all* publications, the user has had since 1968 *Statistical News* [B 24]. This appears quarterly and each issue has several articles dealing with a subject in depth, and shorter notes on other topics. New publications are usually described either in an article or a note, and the periodical enables readers to keep in touch with developments in official statistics. Every issue contains a cumulative index covering the last nine issues.

The indexes and lists of sources at the back of several of the publications described later in this review can also tell the user what publications to consult on a given subject—for example those in the *Annual Abstract* [QRL 2] and *Social Trends* [QRL 17]—and they thus perform something of the function of a guide. The CSO also publishes a brief pamphlet—*Government Statistics, a Brief Guide to Sources* [B 101], listing the main regular publications.

Though it is not strictly a guide, it is worth mentioning that *National Accounts Statistics— Sources and Methods* [B 17] can often be used as such. It lists the numerous sources used in the compilation of the national accounts, many of which are published, and can put the user on the track of figures on a specific subject.

Most of the guides mentioned above are concerned primarily with official publications, and deal only incidentally, if at all, with the non-official material discussed in Section 1.4. The *List of Principal Statistical Series* [B 15] relates almost entirely to official statistics, but it appears that the CSO's forthcoming *Guide to Statistics* will

be rather wider as it will cover statistics published by:

(a) well-known trade associations, professional societies, institutes, voluntary and non-profit-making bodies, and

(b) some UK publications containing important primary data not reproduced in official or semi-official sources.

The list of sources at the back of the *Annual Abstract of Statistics* [QRL 2] refers to a few non-official publications but *Social Trends* [QRL 17] refers to more; *Britain—an Official Handbook* [QRL 3] also lists non-official as well as official sources in its full bibliography. *Statistical News* [B 24] describes a limited number of new non-official publications, and one or two of the specialized official guides listed in the bibliography also include some, e.g. [B 1, 6 and 11].

1.5.2 *Unofficial guides, commentaries, etc.* A number of these are listed in the bibliography, and a few additional comments may be made here. Kendall [B 37] can still be useful in spite of the time that has elapsed since its publication, especially for the more historical type of research. It will eventually be superseded by the series of reviews of which this is one (see [B 24], Aug. 1970, p. 27). Until all these have appeared, parts of the articles will still be of service. Harvey [B 34] and Wills [B 43] are the most comprehensive general surveys of what is available, and these may be supplemented by Edwards [B 32] and the substantial chapter in Fletcher [B 33]. On the use of statistics, Devons [B 31] remains useful in the economic sphere, complemented by the practical approach of Nicholson [B 41] and Lewes [B 38] among more recent books; in the social sphere, Halsey [QRL 37] is outstanding.

As one would expect, the unofficial guides cover non-official statistics more fully than official guides do. Kendall [B 37] included non-official statistics in his scope, as will the companion reviews to this one which will gradually replace

---

* This committee was set up in 1947 'to promote closer co-operation between the universities and government departments' and, as one aspect of this aim, to inform departments of the needs of research workers ([B 68], p. 17). It has issued no publications since 1961, and has now split into two separate committees for economic research and social research respectively. The winding up of the committee was recommended in 1965 by the Heyworth Committee on Social Studies ([B 116], p. 56). On the committee generally, see Feery in Staveley and Piggott [B 105].

the chapters of Kendall. Among the other guides listed in the bibliography, Harvey [B 34] and Wills [B 43] mention most non-official sources, but there is no really comprehensive guide to them.

1.6 Methodological Information on Official Statistics

The user of statistics can scarcely have too much in the way of explanatory matter. Carter and Roy, writing in 1953 ([B 29], p. 138) complained of 'the official failure to provide enough information about the methods of compilation of various statistical series' but very much more is published now than was published when they wrote. It is however very scattered, and it is to be hoped that the forthcoming *Guide to Current Official Statistics* will include references to descriptions of statistical series. The notes on individual general sources later in this review mention the presence of useful explanatory matter if it is included. Among the various other places where such matter may be found are the following:

Bank of England Quarterly Bulletin††
Department of Employment Gazette [QRL 6]
Economic Progress Report (Information Division of the Treasury) [B 66]
Economic Trends [QRL 9]
Financial Statistics—Supplement on Notes and Definitions [B 147] published annually with the April issue
Guides to Official Sources [B 1 and B 9–13]
Housing and Construction Statistics—Notes and Definitions Supplement [B 151], annual
Monthly Digest of Statistics—Supplement of Definitions and Explanatory Notes [QRL 11A], published with the January issue, annually
Social Trends [QRL 17]
Statistical News [B 24]
Studies in Official Statistics. A series of publications on various topics numbering so far twenty-one in the main series, plus five in the research series. Items [B 1 and 15–23] in the

bibliography are in this series, and there are also *inter alia* accounts of the indexes of retail prices and production.

Trade and Industry
Reports of various committees of inquiry: some with a purely statistical remit such as the Retail Prices Index Advisory Committee, the working party on employment statistics, and the committees on criminal and judicial statistics; and others which survey the statistics in their fields as part of their task—for example the Radcliffe Committee on the Working of the Monetary System, the Crowther Committee on Consumer Credit and the Robens Committee on Safety and Health at Work.

Various specific methodological publications such as the *Handbooks* on the *Family Expenditure Surveys* [B 146] and on the *Public Expenditure White Papers* [B 161].

One important class of methodological material is classifications. Those applicable to various subjects will be dealt with in the separate reviews in this series. A reference to the *Standard Industrial Classification* is given in the bibliography [B 93], and those to other classifications will eventually be found in companion reviews—e.g. classifications of overseas trade and tariffs, occupations and diseases.

1.7 Statistics in Non-statistical Publications

The reports and evidence of Royal Commissions and committees of inquiry have long been important sources of statistics. Over recent years a number of developments have tended to increase their usefulness in this respect. Some have appointed statistical advisers, for example the Radcliffe Committee on the Working of the Monetary System and the Robbins Committee on Higher Education. Some have had teams of research workers attached to them, either seconded from the civil service or directly recruited. Special surveys have been undertaken, carried out either by the committee's own staff, the Government Social Survey or outside research organizations.

Special studies have been commissioned, and substantial pieces of research have been carried out, often by academic experts. All this is a great change from conditions previously prevailing. When a sub-committee of the House of Commons Estimates Committee wanted in 1965 to carry out a small survey costing £85 it was dependent on funds provided from a private foundation for doing so ([B 85], p. v). It is said that this parsimonious attitude on the part of the authorities was ended by the refusal of certain prominent persons to act as chairmen of commissions or committees, unless they were properly staffed and had adequate funds for research. The old sort of commission proceeded almost entirely by considering the memoranda submitted and by hearing oral evidence from witnesses. It had a secretary and if it was lucky an assistant secretary. Within these limitations it often did a good job, largely because of the work of the secretary. The procedure was however slow and no substantial research could be undertaken. (There were exceptions to this, such as the Royal Commission on Population.)

The evidence of Select Committees has grown more voluminous in the past few years, perhaps partly as a result of their opening their oral hearings to the public and sometimes going on circuit. They also have employed specialist advisers, and the first Select Committee to do this in recent years was that on government statistical services [B 69]. An example of a Select Committee report partly in the statistical field is that on the population of the UK, of May 1971, from the Select Committee on Science and Technology. Statistical researchers are likely to find that recent major reports are more rewarding, both in their statistical basis and in the volume and quality of their supporting documents—evidence, appendices, research studies and so on. The indexes to reports of Royal Commissions and major committees of inquiry are usually good, and there is sometimes a separately published index to the evidence of Royal Commissions. The indexes to Select Committee reports, on

the other hand, are usually sketchy with little attempt to index the content of the evidence. Users can more often find the figures they want by consulting the list of memoranda near the beginning of reports.

Two particular bodies should be mentioned whose reports may be useful to the researcher—the Monopolies Commission and the National Board for Prices and Incomes (PIB, wound up in 1971). Both these organizations have produced a succession of reports on different subjects, rather than the once-for-all reports of committees of inquiry, and both have adopted a statistical approach, where appropriate, to the subjects referred to them. The PIB sometimes published separate statistical supplements to its reports—as Command Papers, like the reports themselves—and a full list of its reports is contained in a *Supplement* to its Fifth and Final General Report [B 80]. See also [B 47].

Certain economic planning documents also serve as statistical sources for their periods, and references to the *National Plan*, and to plans for Scotland, Wales and Northern Ireland are given in the QRL [QRL 42, 43, 44 and 46].

1.8 Annual Reports of Nationalized Industries and Government Departments

Annual reports of public corporations and government departments were formerly a major source of statistics, but their importance is declining. It was mentioned above that the nationalized industries now publish their annual reports themselves instead of via HMSO (see 1.3.1). If recent reports are compared with those in the early days of nationalization, it will be apparent that, with some exceptions, there has been a great decrease in the amount and range of material published. It is also noteworthy that at a time when more and more companies in the private sector are reporting half-yearly, one of the only two public boards which once did so has ceased the practice.

Some government departments have never

published annual reports, but formerly a fair number did publish substantial reports with an important statistical element. Several factors have affected them:

1. Some never resumed after the war—e.g. that on the army.
2. Some ceased when departments were amalgamated. There were no reports on overseas aid during the period when the Ministry of Overseas Development was part of the Foreign and Commonwealth Office.* The Department of the Environment has produced no reports in succession to those of the Ministry of Housing and Local Government. Much earlier, the report on civil aviation vanished when the subject was taken over by the Ministry of Transport.
3. Reduced frequency. The Ministry of Housing's last reports covered two years, whereas earlier ones had been annual.
4. Separation of the statistical tables. To prevent the Ministry of Housing's figures becoming too stale, they were hived off into a separate
‡ publication (now discontinued), and the same thing has happened—with the parent publication remaining annual—with *Statistics of Education*†† and *Inland Revenue Statistics*††. There can be advantages in this course, as in the last two cases the amount of information published has increased.
5. Shrinkage. Again the Ministry of Housing is an instance and the chapters reviewing special subjects, which used to be such a useful feature, ceased to appear; the report of the DES has contracted to a fraction of its former length and has ceased to be a parlia-
‡ mentary paper. The annual report on Wales has also been greatly cut, and now has virtually no statistics. The DHSS still publishes a substantial report (with the statistics now hived off), but its size is much

smaller than the total of the three reports of its predecessor bodies. (The report of the Ministry of Pensions and National Insurance had already been cut in 1966.) Though not an annual report, the *Supply Estimates*†† are another instance of shrinkage, having been cut once in 1962 and again more drastically in 1974. In consequence much valuable detail has now been lost. The *Memorandum on the Estimates*†† lost one of its most useful features in 1972—a detailed table on civil service salaries—and in 1974 was changed radically for the fourth time in twenty years.

6. 'An economy measure.' This was the reason put forward for the cessation of reports of the Ministries of Works and Labour. (However the latter does publish its *Gazette* [QRL 6].) The same justification would no doubt have been given for the dropping of the reports on *Colonial Territories* [B 119] and *Industry and Employment in Scotland* [QRL 24].

Certain departments publish annual reports on some aspects of their work, e.g. the Home Office and the Departments of Trade and Industry, but on reports covering all activities the situation is at present as follows. Substantial reports are produced only by the Scottish departments, Civil Service Department, DHSS, Customs and Excise and Inland Revenue and rather shorter ones by the
‡ DES and the Welsh Office. Some important areas of activity are covered only thinly or not at all.

1.9 Statistics on the UK in Publications of International Organizations

In general the publications of international organizations are excluded from the scope of this review. It is however worthwhile for the researcher to bear in mind that he can sometimes find information on this country in international publications that is not available in national ones, and this can specially apply to historical inquiries. A few examples will serve to illustrate the point:

* There were however the *UK Memorandum to the Development Assistance Committee of the OECD* [B 131] and brief annual articles in *Economic Trends* [QRL 9].

Retail prices of food. Available since November 1967 in *Ministry of Labour/Department of Employment Gazette* [QRL 6]. An earlier source is the *Yearbook of Labour Statistics* (International Labour Office) [B 172] up to 1958, and subsequently the *Bulletin of Labour Statistics* [B 135], also produced by the ILO.

Tenure of agricultural holdings. 1950 *World Census of Agriculture* [B 164], published by the Food and Agriculture Organization.

Average percentage external tariff. *International Trade* [B 153], 1952. (The General Agreement on Tariffs and Trade.)

UK external trade by continent. Sometimes the user would be better advised to use *Direction of Trade* [B 142] (International Monetary Fund and International Bank for Reconstruction and Development) than UK national statistics, for example if he wanted a run of figures of UK trade with the continent of Africa, an aggregate that is not shown in the national publications.

1.10 General Statistical Publications on Cities and Regions

These are also regarded as outside the scope of this review. It may be worth mentioning that Greater London, Cheshire, Birmingham, Humberside ‡and Glasgow produce compilations of statistics, and there are possibly others. The regional plans, studies and other documents produced by economic planning councils often include figures. These are sometimes published by HMSO, and sometimes by the councils direct. Plans produced for town and country planning purposes can also be useful. These also are sometimes published by HMSO but more often by the council concerned.

1.11 Locating Statistical Material

Once the user has identified the title of the publication he wants, how does he set about getting hold of it? If he wants his own copy of an official publication he can order it through HMSO after con-sulting the indexes and catalogues described above. If he wants to consult it in a library, he should find his path eased by a project carried out between 1967 and 1972 by the Committee of Librarians and Statisticians, on behalf of the Library Association and the Royal Statistical Society. Publications associated with this project are listed in the bibliography—[B 60, 67, 84, 97, 98, 99]. The *Board of Trade Journal* article [B 60] shows which of ninety-one centres outside London have copies of each of fifty-eight basic sources. (The 319 libraries surveyed were public, university and technical college libraries.) The *Union List* [B 99] deals with a much fuller range of titles, and with all the principal libraries which have formally organized collections of statistics, and 'to which there is comprehensive or conditional right of access to research workers or to the public at large'. The user of the union list can identify from it the most convenient library at which he can consult the source he wants, and the list shows how far back libraries hold series. The libraries covered are public, university, government and professional associations' libraries.

The other main publication of the project—*Economic Statistics Collections* [B 67]—is probably likely to be rather less useful. It covers business firms, trade and other associations and trade unions, and lists 296 collections to which some public access may be allowed in certain circumstances; of these, 164 are in London. Unlike the *Union List*, which has details of holdings of individual titles, *Economic Statistics Collections* has only an indication of the broad subject groups on which the collection have material. Ten of these are distinguished, and there is also a group called 'general and miscellaneous'. The entry for each collection also shows: the name of the person to whom inquiries should be directed, the address, whether overseas statistical publications are taken, and whether only current statistics are kept or older ones as well. Both this compilation and the *Union List* [B 99] could be very useful in informing the user of statistical collections, of the existence of which he might otherwise remain in ignorance.

There are also two non-bibliographical aids to help the user locate and use official statistics to the best advantage—the Press and Information Service of the CSO and the Statistics and Market Intelligence Library of the Department of Industry. The latter is open to the general public, has a large public reading room and has facilities for typing, calculating and photo-copying. It has large holdings of publications on economic statistics generally and on overseas trade statistics in particular. Its facilities are described in *Government Statistical Services—A Brief Guide to Sources* [B 101], which also lists enquiry points in the main government departments, manned by members of the GSS whom users can consult if they cannot find a source for the statistics they require.

2 General Sources of Statistics

2.1 Most of the rest of this review is devoted to descriptions of general statistical sources. These are arranged in four groups:

1. Current regular serial publications.
2. Discontinued publications, of which a selection is dealt with more briefly.
3. Books and publications which appear irregularly.
4. Supplement on recent new series.

The order is the same as in the Quick Reference List and the numbering also corresponds.

The emphasis is on current material but some historical material has been included as well. As it would have been tedious to set out the subjects included in each source in all the individual notes, the subject coverage of many of them is set out in Table I at the end of the review. Sources included in this table have the sign † after their titles at the beginning of each note.

The geographical coverage of the sources is the United Kingdom unless indicated otherwise, but sources covering separate constituent countries of the United Kingdom have also been included; there are none on England alone. There has never been complete uniformity, but the general pattern has been that each country has both a purely statistical publication and a publication combining text with statistics. The collection of statistics tends to follow the pattern of administration, so the statistics published in the separate-country publications may vary with the degree of delegation of power to those countries.* The largest number of functions is delegated to Northern Ireland, the next largest to Scotland and

the smallest to Wales. One must also bear in mind that the *amount* of delegation has increased over the last twenty years or so with more functions being transferred to Scottish departments and the Welsh Office. These considerations partly govern whether, and for what periods, one should consult national (UK) sources or country sources for Northern Ireland, Scotland and Wales.

National general publications in this country are mostly purely statistical in character, whereas in some countries, for example Canada [B 136], Australia [B 159] and New Zealand [B 157], the statistical departments produce *Official Yearbooks* combining statistics and text in what is for some purposes a useful manner. In *Britain—an Official Handbook* [QRL 3], compiled by the Central Office of Information, the emphasis is on the text, but the reader's understanding of the statistics it contains is often helped by the commentary. *Social Trends* [QRL 17] also combines text and figures as does the new *Local Government Trends* [QRL 39].

Such general reference books as *Whitaker's Almanack*, the *Statesman's Year Book* and the *Municipal Year-book* are excluded from the list of general sources. This is not because I underrate their usefulness, but because their scope is not limited to statistics. I have however included *British Political Facts* [QRL 32] as this is possibly less widely known.

Current Regular Serial Publications

‡**2.2.1** *Abstract of Regional Statistics*† [QRL 1]. This series owed its origin to the keen interest in regional questions current at the time of the preparation of the *National Plan* [QRL 42]. The first issue, for 1965, contained forty-three tables,

---

* For example the Scottish *Abstract* [QRL 15] gives figures of divorces, whereas the Welsh *Digest* [QRL 8] cannot as there are no separate civil judicial statistics for Wales.

whereas the 1973 issue has ninety. The first issue gave the impression of a fairly random collection of the tables which could be found on a regional basis in other publications, and which were included whether it was useful to republish them or not. Only half the tables in it used standard regions, so that comparability between the tables was limited. (But of course on some subjects, for example fuel, there was no alternative to using the boundaries already in use.) Eleven different regional classifications were listed, and for full details of them the user would have had to refer to five publications besides the *Abstract of Regional Statistics*. There was no map, and only eight tables were not published elsewhere.

The publication was subsequently greatly improved and enlarged. In the 1973 issue, eighteen tables consist of material not published elsewhere, and only four (all on the fuel industries) deal with areas other than standard regions. The regional estimates of the gross domestic product are a notable addition to the 1973 issue. The *Abstract of Regional Statistics* contains some tables for which national figures are not in the *Annual Abstract* [QRL 2], for example those on household consumption of main foods and on consumer durables in use. It can therefore sometimes usefully be consulted for national as well as regional figures. A map is included, as is a list of the composition of sub-divisions of regions, in terms both of local authority areas and of the areas covered by employment exchanges. There is also an index of sources. Four batches of tables—on population, gross domestic product, incomes and household surveys—have explanatory notes; for other tables the user should consult the supplement to the *Monthly Digest of Statistics* [QRL 11A].

2.2.2. The *Annual Abstract of Statistics*† [QRL 2] is the most important annual statistical publication for the United Kingdom. As the *Statistical Abstract for the United Kingdom*, it was first published in 1854, and the first issue covered the years 1840 to 1853. After the eighty-third issue, published in

1940 and covering the years 1924 to 1938, there is a break in the series because of the war. However the first post-war edition, published in 1948, gives figures for all the war years, and it may be supplemented by the *Statistical Digest of the War* [QRL 34]. The 1948 edition differs from its predecessors in the following ways. It was compiled by the CSO whereas earlier issues had been compiled by the Board of Trade; it appeared in a larger format than the pre-war issues; consequently it could no longer be a parliamentary paper but was issued as a non-parliamentary publication.

As will be seen from Table I, the *Annual Abstract* has figures on almost every subject, mostly derived from government departments and their publications. There is a very useful list of sources at the back giving references which the user can follow up to obtain more detail or more recent figures. There is a full index, a selection of conversions of units of measurement and a list of headings used for the *Standard Industrial Classification* [B 93]. Often somebody looking for detailed statistics on a certain subject can find them by: first, consulting the alphabetical index to get the relevant table number and secondly, consulting the list of sources to find for that table the name of the detailed source publication. As far as possible tables relate to the United Kingdom, but a considerable number of tables refer to Great Britain or England and Wales. There is also a fair number of tables on Scotland and Northern Ireland, even though there are separate statistical publications on those countries. There is often no way round having separate country tables: for example a different legal system prevents the amalgamation of Scottish criminal statistics with those for England and Wales. (Sometimes however the separate tables stem from the different departmental origins of the figures, for example the tables of fish landings in the *Abstract* up to the 1967 issue, for which rather unnecessarily separate tables were included for Scotland and England and Wales.)

On many of the series in the *Abstract*, methodological information can be found in the *Supplement of Definitions and Explanatory Notes* issued each January with the *Monthly Digest of Statistics* [QRL 11A]. The 1972 issue of this *Supplement* contained for the first time a list of sources linking tables in the *Monthly Digest* and the *Abstract*. On financial series the user is referred to the similar supplement to *Financial Statistics* [B 147] published with each April issue of that publication. Of the fifteen chapters of the *Abstract*, four whole chapters and sections of three others have explanatory notes before the statistical tables. On the whole the tables themselves are rather sparsely supplied with footnotes. It is true that an excess of footnotes can mar the appearance of a page and intimidate the user (though a surplus can be transferred to the back of the book as in *Social Trends* [QRL 17]), but the absence of a key footnote can be misleading. For example, for some years (but not now), the *Abstract*'s table on juvenile delinquency in England and Wales showed a spurious reduction in crime between 1963 and 1964, in fact accounted for by the raising of the age of legal responsibility. To take a further example, the *Abstract* used to have tables showing UK total trade with 'the Commonwealth' over a period of nine years. The membership of 'the Commonwealth' changes, but it was unclear if the figures reflected its changing composition or if they referred to a *constant* collection of countries belonging at the time the table was compiled. Figures of trade with the Commonwealth have now been dropped even though one could expect the information to be of interest, and in fact the respective amounts of British trade with the Commonwealth and the EEC are exactly the sort of figures one would hope to find in the *Abstract*. (In other respects, area and country detail on overseas trade has been expanded.)

Another problem concerns the 'marrying' of figures from the *Abstract* with those in other publications. Sometimes it is necessary to update an *Abstract* table with figures from a more recent source, often one shown as the source publication in the list at the back; in some cases the *Abstract* table is more *recent* than the source publication. It can be baffling if the figures in the two do not correspond (though revisions for the most recent period are to be expected), and in such circumstances one may conclude that it is unwise to link series. (This problem arose for example with statistics of migration.) Where there is a discrepancy between figures in the *Abstract* and those in the source publication quoted, an explanatory note could reassure users.

The *Abstract* provides the answers to many statistical enquiries for the period it covers, but omits some series which seem to me to merit inclusion. There are no retail prices of actual commodities (as opposed to index-numbers) though the International Labour Office has long published such figures for this country; rates are given of direct taxation but no specimen rates of indirect taxes; earnings were shown by industry up to 1971 for white-collar workers but not for the more numerous manual workers: currently there are no figures in money terms of earnings by industry at all; there are no figures of local elections, and the table on general elections is rather inadequate. It has no figures of votes by party: the figures of seats by party differ slightly from those in the most authoritative source and oversimplify the political scene, apparently labelling Mr Ramsay MacDonald a Conservative in 1931. The *Abstract* contains no figures from the National Food Survey and has only recently started to include the percentage rate of unemployment even though this is a much used economic indicator. Economic statistics predominate in the contents of the *Abstract*, and *Social Trends* [QRL 17] supplements it in the field of social statistics.

When the Estimates Sub-Committee put it to a CSO witness that the range of the contents of the *Abstract* should be widened, he replied that its size had to be limited to keep the price down ([B 69], q. 1314). This point is possibly less convincing when one does some price comparisons.

The US *Abstract*, with three times as many tables as the British, sells for about the same price in hardback as the British in paperback; and the Norwegian and Danish Yearbooks are both cheaper than the UK *Abstract* in spite of being larger. These criticisms do not detract from the many merits of the *Annual Abstract*. It is because it is the most important single British official statistical publication that one expects from it a high standard and in most respects one is not disappointed.

2.2.3 *Britain—An Official Handbook* [QRL 3] is prepared annually by the Reference Division of the Central Office of Information (COI). It was first published in 1946, but to start with was distributed only overseas. On the recommendation of the Inter-Departmental Committee for Social and Economic Research, it was put on sale in this country and issues for 1954 and subsequent years have been generally available. It is now a handbook of over 500 pages and the 1974 edition is very reasonably priced at £2·10. This edition consists of twenty-two chapters containing a total of thirty-five statistical tables; there are also eleven diagrams of a statistical nature. These details however give a misleadingly low impression of the statistical content of the book, as the text is packed with statistics on a very wide range of subjects. This combination of figures and text can often be more illuminating than a purely statistical compilation, as is shown by the *Official Yearbooks* published by the governments of Canada and New Zealand [B 136, B 157].

The *Official Handbook* is not of course only a statistical publication, as it gives, in the words of the preface, 'a factual account of the administration and economy . . . and describes the activities of many of the national institutions'. It has a good index and a full bibliography which is by no means confined to official publications, as is mostly the case with works compiled in the statistical departments. Similarly some of the figures it gives, such as the circulation of individual newspapers

or the votes cast at elections analysed by party, are not published in purely statistical official publications, and it covers subjects such as religion, leisure and the arts, which the statistical publications tend to neglect. On many subjects covered by the *Handbook*, the COI publishes separate reference pamphlets containing material closely related to the material in the *Handbook*, but in some cases going into much more detail. Some of these are substantial, for example those on social services, invisible exports, and the education system, and contain their own bibliographies and statistical tables; they are however less frequently updated than the *Handbook*. Users of the *Handbook* interested in only one of its chapters obviously find it more convenient to acquire only a pamphlet, if one is published on their subject. The pamphlets are listed in the bibliography of the *Handbook* and in Sectional List No. 53 of HMSO. To mention a further COI publication, *Britain in Brief* [B 134] is an excellent sixty-page pamphlet with a selection of basic figures and a great bargain at 12p.

The COI makes no claim that the *Handbook* or its other publications are anything but secondary sources, but as such they are extremely useful, serve as a valuable start to the researcher beginning to look into a subject, and guide him to where he can find more detail.

2.2.4 *The British Economy—Key Statistics*† [QRL 4] is published at intervals by Times Newspapers for the London and Cambridge Economic Service (LCES). Issues have appeared entitled 1900–62, 1900–64, 1900–66 and 1900–70. These publications supplement the *Bulletins* of the LCES [QRL 25] which have appeared in various forms at different periods, and which formerly contained several tables corresponding to some of those in *Key Statistics*. Until the end of 1951, the *Bulletin* was an independent quarterly publication and twenty-nine annually numbered volumes were produced in that form. From March 1952 until the end of 1965 it appeared as a quarterly insert in the *Times Review of Industry* [B 130]. To give an indication of its statistical content—the December 1965 issue contained eight tables, including about 130 series all told, with figures for a continuous run of nine recent years, five selected years between 1913 and 1948 and quarters for the most recent three years. The subjects covered included national income, production, productivity, transport, employment, wages, prices, investment, overseas trade, finance and balance of payments. Some time before the demise of the *Times Review of Industry*, the *Bulletin* transferred to *The Times* newspaper, where it still appears, but without the regular statistical tables which once accompanied it. (It is now half-yearly and separate reprints are available.) Thus *Key Statistics* is the remaining statistical product of the LCES, and a very useful product it is.

Its great virtue is to show long runs of years covering the whole of this century, drawing on different sources, indicating major and minor changes of definition (by different thicknesses of line), but making an attempt at a continuous series if at all possible. For some figures the LCES has not been afraid to make its own rough estimates, and these are shown in brackets. In the issue for 1900–70, there are fifteen pages of tables of which thirteen are entirely, and one largely, on the United Kingdom and one is on the USA. With up to seventeen series on each page, there are thus well over 200 series on the British economy, and where the information is available, there is a figure for each of the seventy years of the period covered. (The table on external finance includes only three years before 1920 because of the paucity of information.) The 1900–70 issue uses decimal currency throughout, and the index numbers all have 1963 as 100 (often, as with the *National Institute Economic Review* [QRL 12], a purely arithmetical conversion; i.e. the weights refer to a different year). Some information will be found in *Key Statistics* [QRL 4] that is not in the *Annual Abstract* [QRL 2]—e.g. specimen rates of indirect taxation. A useful feature of the notes is a list of tax changes that occurred otherwise than at budgets.

There are seven pages giving notes and sources, plus an index, and the references are generally sufficient to take the user back without difficulty to the original source if necessary, and enable him to update series himself. For recent years the sources are mostly official publications, but for earlier years, when fewer statistics were published, it was necessary to draw on a wide variety of different sources—academic books, articles in learned journals, a doctoral thesis, a 1925 Report of a Royal Commission, and unpublished estimates. The wide range of source material used no doubt stems from the different specialities of the members of the editorial committee—collectively covering a far wider field than an individual editor could.

2.2.5 *British Labour Statistics Year Book*† [QRL 5]. The Department of Employment under its various names has always been among the government departments with a good record of publishing statistical information, to the great benefit of research workers and other users. The original impetus to the Board of Trade (which was then in charge of labour matters) came from a resolution of the House of Commons in 1886, and *Abstracts of Labour Statistics* [B 117] were published from 1894 onwards. Publication was at first annual, but became usually triennial between the wars and the last issue of the series (the twenty-second) appeared in 1937.* The series was not resumed after the Second World War, but the White Paper of 1962 *Incomes Policy: the Next Step* (Cmnd. 1626) resulted in the quarterly *Statistics on Incomes, Prices, Employment and Production* [QRL 26], which covered some of the field of the *Abstracts*. This ran for twenty-nine issues until June 1969, and when it was in its turn discontinued, an annual volume of labour statistics was promised to replace it.

* For a list of *Abstracts of Labour Statistics* see *Labour Statistics —Guide to Official Sources* [B9], p. 66.

The first such annual volume, *British Labour Statistics; Year Book 1969* [QRL 5] was preceded by *British Labour Statistics: Historical Abstract 1886–1968* [QRL 31]. The latter is essentially an abstract of the statistics which appeared in the publications named in the previous paragraph, in the *Department of Employment Gazette* [QRL 6] under its successive titles, and in associated reports on particular surveys. The *Historical Abstract* contains 400 pages of tables, is amply provided with explanatory matter and is in general very well produced.

Year Books have now been published for each year for the period 1969–73 inclusive, and it is intended to continue the sequence. The *Year Books* bring together all the main statistics produced by the Department of Employment for the reference year and, where appropriate, include time series for up to ten years. There are some graphs, and appendices reproduce articles originally published in the *Gazette* [QRL 6]. The subjects covered by the main tables mostly are the same in each issue, but those covered by the articles vary from issue to issue so that it is worth consulting more than one. For example the *Historical Abstract* has material on shift working and the size of manufacturing establishments, which has not so far been updated; similarly the 1969 *Year Book* has tables on labour costs. Profit sharing and co-partnership—a regular topic in pre-war days—seem to have dropped out altogether, presumably because they are no longer regarded as of much interest. Later figures for the *Year Book's* tables are to be found in the *Gazette* itself, and these will in their turn be included in subsequent *Year Books*.

‡**2.2.6** *The Department of Employment Gazette*† [QRL 6] has appeared monthly under a succession of different titles since 1893. It is the main periodical for the publication of statistics in the field covered by the Department, but certain figures are also given in the *Monthly Digest of Statistics* [QRL 11] and *Economic Trends* [QRL 9]. Most of the statistical material in the *Gazette* is now col-

lected annually in the *British Labour Statistics Yearbook* [QRL 5], and this, together with *British Labour Statistics: Historical Abstract 1886–1968* [QRL 31], is usually a more convenient source to use than the *Gazette* for the periods they cover. (For the period 1962–9, many of the figures will also be found in *Statistics on Incomes, Prices, Employment and Production* [QRL 26].) The statistical series contained in the *Gazette* are described (or are to be described) in other reviews in this series, so only a general description of the arrangement of the *Gazette* will be given here.

Each issue is currently arranged in four sections: special articles, 'News and Notes', 'Monthly Statistics' and 'Statistical Series'. It is however important for the user to realize that statistics and items of statistical interest are included in all the sections. The first part contains *inter alia*: figures that are collected less frequently than monthly, often with a commentary on them, such as the annual employment series analysed by industry and region, and the preliminary results of the *New Earnings Survey*†† and *Family Expenditure Survey*†† which appear in the form of articles before coming out later as books; accounts of new statistical series or changes in old ones, giving details of methods of compilation, weighting patterns and so on; and some regular quarterly figures, for example those on accidents at work. The second section ('News and Notes') includes notes of changes in statistical series too small to justify a full article, and some regular quarterly series, for example those on redundancy payments and on expenditure on unemployment benefit. The third section ('Monthly Statistics') covers the same subjects every month. but once a quarter has more analyses of unemployment. It is also worth mentioning that the table on unemployment in local areas sometimes contains local employment figures for separate localities which are not published elsewhere. (In 1974 these were not included in the *Gazette* but were obtainable from the Department.) The fourth section ('Statistical Series') usually contains the same tables every month. This section has an introductory note at the beginning, a number of graphs at various points, and a list of definitions of terms at the end.

The *Gazette* has an annual index; users should bear in mind that on some subjects they may have to consult the indexes for several years before finding relevant articles. Examples of such subjects are shift working or labour costs on which the Department collects information infrequently. For the period which it covers, *Labour Statistics— Guide to Official Sources* [B 9] is invaluable in listing articles on these more elusive subjects; articles could also be found through the *Annual Reports of the Ministry of Labour* [B 118] until the latter ceased with the issue for 1960.

In May 1966 a fresh periodical *Changes in Rates of Wages and Hours of Work* [B 139] was started to include information previously given in the *Gazette*. (It did not appear during the 'pay-freezes' of 1966 and 1972–3 when by definition no changes were possible.)

Several of the statistical series from the *Gazette* appear first in the form of press notices issued by the Department, and are in the newspapers the following day. As is mentioned in the commentary on *Economic Trends* [QRL 9] (2.2.9), these notices are listed there; the list is also given in *Trade and Industry* [QRL 18].

2.2.7 *Digest of Statistics* (*Northern Ireland*)† [QRL 7]. A twice-yearly publication, it has increased from ninety-eight tables in the first issue (March 1954) to 159 tables in that for March 1974. Almost all the tables are supplied by departments of the government of Northern Ireland, the exceptions being material contributed by the Inland Revenue, Meteorological Office, Post Office and Department of Employment. Department of Employment figures on wage-rates and retail prices in the UK are included in the absence of series for Northern Ireland on its own. The tables on social service expenditure are accompanied by a full introductory note, but there is

otherwise little in the way of explanatory matter. There is no index and the list of sources is fairly brief; the latter may however be supplemented by the full bibliography in the *Ulster Yearbook* [QRL 19]. One function of the *Digest* is that it serves as a source for material needed to convert figures for Great Britain into figures for the United Kingdom. One perhaps wants to bring up to date a UK table from say the *Annual Abstract of Statistics* [QRL 2], finds that the figures in the main current source cover only Great Britain, and has to add on figures for Northern Ireland to make the coverage the same. It is therefore important that the scope of series should be kept in line, and this is usually the case.

‡**2.2.8** *Digest of Welsh Statistics*† [QRL 8]. This annual publication started in 1954 with eighty tables and had more than doubled in size to reach 212 tables by the 1972/3 edition. Before the foundation of the Welsh Office the *Digest* was sponsored successively by the Home Office, from 1954 to 1956, and by the Ministry of Housing and Local Government, from 1957 to 1961. The first four issues were published in conjunction with the annual *Reports on Wales and Monmouthshire*, shown under its current title as [QRL 20]; later editions came out independently because of timing difficulties. The *Digest* has been notably expanded in various years. The 1959 issue was brought more into line with the Scottish *Digest* [QRL 21] and *Annual Abstract* [QRL 2], and an index was introduced for the first time in the 1966 issue. In the 1970 issue, perhaps partly in response to criticism made in *Statistical News* [B 49], there was a reappearance of various statistics on health which had formerly appeared in the *Annual Report* of the DHSS††, and which had vanished from that Report when the Department ceased to be responsible for health matters in Wales. In the 1971 issue there was a new section on social security, and estimates of the Welsh gross domestic product and expenditure were first included; and in the 1972/3 issue there were *inter alia* additional information on

education, a summary of the data from the 1971 population census for each Welsh local authority, and a table and map of the new local authorities after reorganization. One problem with the *Digest* relates to the non-disclosure of information, and figures for some industries are left out because their publication would disclose the production figures for individual firms.

A good feature worthy of extension where appropriate is the comparison made in some tables between Wales and either Great Britain, the United Kingdom or England and Wales, for example in the tables on pupils staying on at school after fifteen, activity rates and distribution of the employed population among industries. There is no list of sources and no explanatory matter other than footnotes, nor any references to where explanations might be found. The *Digest* does however have a map, an index and a schedule of the composition of geographical subdivisions in terms of administrative and employment exchange areas.

The *Annual Report* on Wales [QRL 20], mentioned above, started with the issue for 1945-6. The first issues had a Statistical Appendix, which forms a source for Welsh statistics before the institution of the *Digest*. When the *Digest* started, the tables were transferred to it, along with some statistical data from the text. The *Annual Report* has since fluctuated in size and in statistical content, rising to a maximum of about 200 pages with the 1968 issue; it has included the statutory annual report on Welsh roads since the 1965 issue. The issues for 1971 onwards are much smaller but completely bilingual. The reader is referred to the *Digest* and to various separate reports for information previously included. *Progress in Wales—Quarterly Summaries of Economic Developments* [B 160] brings some of the information in both the *Digest* and *Annual Report* up to date. This is however not generally published, but is circulated by the Welsh Office to various recipients. The Office would no doubt inform inquirers where it was available for consultation.

‡2.2.9 *Economic Trends*† [QRL 9]. This is a monthly publication, first published in November 1953. Until the end of 1956 it served mainly as a supplement to the *Monthly Digest of Statistics* [QRL 11] for graphs and diagrams. During that period it was therefore mainly useful for people who preferred that form of presentation to unadorned tables. From 1957 it started to include articles and special tables as well as the regular graphs; the first article was concerned with the new quarterly estimates of national income and expenditure. Considerable changes are again planned for *Economic Trends*, and this note is concerned with its contents in mid-1974. The articles now published fall into three categories:

1. Regular quarterly articles on national income and expenditure and on the UK balance of payments. The October national income article has long runs of quarterly figures, as does the September balance of payments article. Until May 1974 there was a regular monthly article on the economic situation by the Treasury; this continues to appear in *Trade and Industry* [QRL 18] and in the *Economic Progress Report* issued by the Information Division of the Treasury.

2. Regular annual articles or tables on various topics, appearing usually in the same month each year, e.g. tables on the national income additional to those in the National Income Blue Book (including some growth triangles with growth rates worked out between any two years in the period covered); the calendars of economic events (see 2.2.12); international comparisons of taxes and social security contributions; and articles on the incidence of taxes and benefits in the UK, showing their redistributive effect.

3. Other articles, which are often reports on pieces of economic or statistical research or introductions to new statistical series.

Selected articles have been reprinted in *New Contributions to Economic Statistics*, of which a new issue appears every two or three years [B 18–23]. A list of articles published in the last two years or so is printed inside the back cover of each issue of *Economic Trends*. Between 1963 and 1967 the *Economic Report* [QRL 23] (see 2.2.23) appeared as a supplement to *Economic Trends*.

Economic Trends also has the following features:

(a) four pages of main economic statistical series, mostly in seasonally adjusted form, covering twelve years or so on a quarterly basis.

(b) a table of measures of variability of some major series (from August 1972, when a complete description of these measures was published).

(c) a list inside the front cover of the dates of publication in the coming month of the main economic figures. These are mostly first published in the form of press notices issued by government departments.

(d) an index of sources of the statistics in the monthly charts and tables in the second half of the publication. More detail and longer runs can be found in the sources given in this index.

2.2.10 The *London Gazette* [QRL 10] may not be thought of as a statistical source, but can just be included in this category. Historically it is much older than any other current publication, having been founded in 1665. It published more statistics before the Second World War than it does now, but it still includes a rather curious collection of figures. The subjects covered include cereal prices, diseases of animals, bankruptcies, the Bank of England weekly return, the note issue of the Scottish banks, and the transactions of the Consolidated and National Loans Funds, including separate monthly figures of payments from the UK Exchequer to the European Economic Community. The *Gazette* appears somewhat intimidating, as does its index, which is quarterly. In the index, one finds references to the statistics

under the names of the body collecting them rather than under the subject, except that bankruptcies go under the heading 'Bankruptcy Acts'. All references to statistics are included in the section of the index headed 'State intelligence'.

2.2.11 *Monthly Digest of Statistics*† [QRL 11]. This is the most useful single general statistical periodical, and if only one such periodical is taken by an institution, this should be the one. It complements the *Annual Abstract* [QRL 2] and, in fields where the coverage overlaps, keeps it up to date. It mostly contain seriess which are available at intervals of less than a year—usually monthly or quarterly. (There are exceptions, for example the estimates of population.) For this reason, figures of national income and expenditure were not included until the start of quarterly estimates. The first issue, for January 1946, contained 108 tables in eleven chapters whereas that for July 1974 had 174 regular tables in nineteen chapters, plus a supplementary table. Besides the general expansion over the period, the *Digest* has shown variations in its contents, though certain series have appeared throughout. In particular the *Digest* once contained much more in the way of detailed figures of employment in separate industries than it does now.

A *Supplement* of definitions and explanatory notes is published annually at the same time as the January issue [QRL 11A]; these definitions also apply, where relevant, to corresponding tables in the *Annual Abstract of Statistics* [QRL 2] and the *Abstract of Regional Statistics* [QRL 1]. This *Supplement* gives for many tables in the *Digest* references to articles and reports where yet more detail may be found on methods of compilation, as well as descriptions of the weighting pattern of index-numbers and so on. A valuable new feature of the *Supplement* from 1972 onwards is an index of sources referring the user both to corresponding tables in the *Annual Abstract* and to the basic sources—usually those in which the information is first published.

At one time, several tables did not appear every month but only at intervals over the year. For example the 1959 *Supplement* listed eight subjects on which tables did not appear monthly. The February issue, up to and including 1959, contained a most useful Summary of Annual Statistics, which collected together in six pages a comprehensive selection of indicators for several years, and served as an abridged interim version of the *Annual Abstract* until the publication of the latter in the following autumn or winter.

A special feature of long standing was the tables on expenditure on the social services, published annually in the May issue until 1971, when it ceased. This series (known as the 'Drage return' after the statistician Geoffrey Drage) extended back for more than fifty years in various forms: from 1919 to 1931 it was a House of Commons paper; from 1932 to 1939 a Command paper; from 1940 to 1950 on a reduced scale a written answer to an 'inspired' parliamentary question; and from 1951 to 1971 it appeared in the May *Monthly Digest*. The scope varied—the tables once included figures of persons benefiting from the expenditure, and the most recent tables covered the UK whereas they once covered Great Britain.

From June 1971, the chapter of the *Digest* on external trade was expanded to include some material formerly included in the monthly *Report on Overseas Trade* [B 126], which had been discontinued. A note at the front of the *Digest* draws attention to new or discontinued tables; changes are usually most numerous at the beginning of a year. Each issue contains a fairly brief alphabetical index. The *Digest* does not contain charts or graphs, which should be sought in other publications, especially *Economic Trends* [QRL 9] and *Social Trends* [QRL 17].

Currently (mid-1974) the *Digest* carries regular supplementary tables on two subjects—population projections and the index of production—with an occasional set of tables on another subject, such as those on foreign and coastwise trade in the April 1974 *Digest*. The supplementary tables appear only

in one issue, and are not repeated subsequently until a year or so later when they are updated. The population projections generally appear in a summer issue and are accompanied by a note setting out the assumptions on which they are based. The tables on the index of production normally appear in the autumn, for example those in the issue for October 1973 which showed the monthly figures for 1968–71, re-based on 1970. Supplementary tables are at present not particularly well signposted; they are mentioned in the introduction to the *Digest* each month with the date of the issue in which they last appeared, but it might be preferable to revert to an earlier practice and mention them also in the alphabetical index of each issue.

The published predecessor of the *Digest* was the monthly *Statistical Summary* [B 129] produced by the Bank of England. (There was an immediate predecessor of the *Digest* during the war which was circulated only inside the government.) One has only to glance at the pre-war issues of this series (containing about twenty tables, on general as well as financial subjects), to see how the *Digest* transformed the scene. Though much of the information in it is available elsewhere, it is invaluable to have it collected in one publication, and in one that appears so frequently.

2.2.12 The *National Institute Economic Review†* [QRL 12] is published by the National Institute of Economic and Social Research. It started in January 1959 and for the first three years appeared every two months; from 1962 onwards it has been published quarterly. All issues have contained an important Statistical Appendix which has varied in size between twenty and thirty tables, and at present (August 1974 issue) includes twenty-five tables. Of these sixteen contain figures on the United Kingdom, and the remainder are international tables. Half of the international tables contain series for the United Kingdom in the context of comparable statistics for other countries. Until the end of 1966 a quarterly statistical supplement was published between issues of the *Review* to bring some of the figures up to date. Detailed definitions and explanatory notes for the tables are published about every two years in the *Review*, and from time to time the *Review* includes articles or notes on specific series explaining such matters as changes in methods of compilation. Many of the other articles in the *Review* are partly statistical in character, notably those containing forecasts for the UK economy. An index to special articles, covering the whole run of the *Review*, appears in each February issue; there is a list of titles of articles that have appeared in about the last four years on the back cover of each issue. A useful feature is the 'calendar of economic events', which was once annual but is now quarterly. The first such calendar covered the period 1955–9, and subsequent calendars appeared in the March or February issue for years up to and including 1969. The May 1970 issue contains the first quarterly calendar. The *Review* calendars complement, rather than directly compete with, the calendars in *Economic Trends* [QRL 9]; the latter, first published in 1969, goes back only to 1964, and goes into more detail on a narrower range of events. The *Review*'s arrangement is primarily chronological, whereas *Economic Trends* sorts events by category and provides useful supporting detail.

The tables in the Statistical Appendix have fairly long runs, with annual figures for up to twelve years and quarterly or monthly figures for the most recent period. Many of the series are index-numbers, and they have been converted to have 1970 as 100 (where this was not the original base), to make comparisons easy. (This conversion is of course purely arithmetical and does not necessarily imply that 1970 weights are used.) As far as possible series are shown seasonally adjusted, a few seasonal adjustments being carried out by the National Institute itself. The Institute includes its own estimates for some series where an official figure is not yet available, and these are shown in italics; the series on output per man hour in manufacturing in the UK is original throughout. The emphasis in the Appendix is on giving information on *changes* in economic variables rather than on absolute levels, for which figures can be found elsewhere.

‡2.2.13 *Northern Ireland Economic Report* [QRL 13]. This has appeared annually since 1964. The predecessor of the series was the *Northern Ireland Economic Survey* (1963, NI Cmd. 453), of which only one appeared; this had thirty-four tables in a statistical appendix plus others in the text. Two other earlier publications on Northern Ireland are listed in the Reference List [QRL 41 and 43]. The 1973 *Economic Report* consisted of an eleven-page commentary with text tables on employment and production, plus a statistical appendix with tables and charts on domestic product, construction, unemployment, agriculture and general economic series. The charts were a new feature of the 1973 issue, which also included for the first time a calendar of economic events for both the UK and Northern Ireland. The 1972 issue included a progress report on the 1970–5 Northern Ireland Development Programme. Fuller discussion of the economy of Northern Ireland will be found in *The Economic Development of Northern Ireland* by T. Wilson, 1965, NI Cmd. 479 and the *Northern Ireland Development Programme 1970–1975*, HMSO, Belfast, non-parl., 1970. An account of official statistics of Northern Ireland is given in *Statistical News* [B 55].

2.2.14 *OECD Economic Survey of the United Kingdom* [QRL 14]. The Organization for Economic Co-operation and Development (OECD) and its predecessor body the OEEC have published economic surveys on each member country (separately) since the early 1950s. Though they are called 'annual' there is not necessarily a survey on all the countries every year. They deal with recent developments in the economy and prospects for the immediate future, with some statistical forecasts. The emphasis tends to be on monetary and financial matters and the balance of payments rather than on, say, industrial aspects. There is a statistical annex with half a dozen tables plus a further dozen or more, and some charts, in the text. These are mostly based on readily available sources, but sometimes incorporate estimates made by the secretariat for the latest periods shown or for the future. The *Survey* for January 1973 also included a calendar of economic events for 1972, plus some appendix tables on activity rates and unemployment. The *Surveys* give in a brief compass an outside view of the British economy with a selection of illustrative figures; there is now no similar document produced by the government. (See below in the note on the *Economic Report* [QRL 23], 2.2.23.) Parts of the *Surveys* are updated by *Economic Outlook* [B 143], published twice yearly by OECD.

2.2.15 *Scottish Abstract of Statistics*† [QRL 15]. A new annual publication starting in 1971, the *Scottish Abstract*, together with the *Scottish Economic Bulletin*, [QRL 16] replaces the *Digest of Scottish Statistics* [QRL 21]. The 1973 issue has 167 tables arranged in nine chapters, and most groups of tables are provided with useful introductory notes. There is a full list of sources, a good index, a schedule of the composition of Scottish planning regions and four maps. At the foot of some tables the name of a source publication is given, and these tables are presumably reprinted in un-changed form from other publications. Most users will find it advantageous to have this material within one cover, and sometimes the *Abstract* gives a longer run of figures than one issue of the source publication.

Compared with the *Digest of Scottish Statistics* the *Abstract* has more material on health, housing, justice and education and on the Family Expenditure Survey. The only tables dropped, compared with the *Digest*, appear to be one on shipping movements and two not very useful tables on the UK national income and on general economic

statistics for the UK. The *Digest* ran from April 1953 to April 1971, and increased from fifty-seven tables in the first issue to eighty-eight in the last. It appeared twice a year, whereas the *Abstract* is annual, but the *Abstract* gives a wider range of information. A selection of the main series of figures is brought up to date every six months in the *Scottish Economic Bulletin* [QRL 16].

2.2.16 *Scottish Economic Bulletin*† [QRL 16]. This appears twice a year and started in the summer of 1971. It fulfils the same function for the Scottish economy as that performed by *Economic Trends* [QRL 9] for the economy of the UK as a whole. Each issue contains a general economic commentary, charts and tables, and there have also been special articles which vary in subject from issue to issue. Examples are: Scottish banks and the new system of credit control, industrial building in Scotland, and the British Steel Corporation's development strategy. Many of the figures are also in the *Scottish Abstract of Statistics* [QRL 15]: those of the Scottish gross domestic product at first appeared only in the *Bulletin*, but are now in the *Abstract* as well. (There is a note on their compilation in the first issue of the *Bulletin*.) A special number appeared in 1973 on North Sea Oil, and the enlarged issue for July 1974 included three items on the subject. This issue also included for the first time a calendar of economic events and a cumulative index to the contents of the series so far. The tables of main economic indicators have long runs of quarterly figures covering about eleven years. On several subjects there are comparisons between Scotland and the whole of Great Britain, for example on earnings, the pattern of employment and gross domestic product per head, and comparisons have also been included with regions of some continental countries in the fields of migration and employment. The charts are accompanied by useful commentaries bringing out their main points. The publication does much to fill the gap left by the discontinuance of the annual White

Paper on *Industry and Employment in Scotland* [QRL 24] which ran from 1946 to 1963 and offered a general survey of the Scottish economy.

‡2.2.17   *Social Trends*† [QRL 17] collects together annually many of the main statistics relevant to social conditions and social policies. When it first appeared in 1970 it indicated a change in direction in two respects on the part of the CSO. First it marked the end of the CSO's hitherto virtually exclusive preoccupation with economic and financial statistics. Secondly, it went very much further to help the user than any previous publication. The resemblance to *Economic Trends* [QRL 9] is not as great as the similarity of name would imply: the latter is a monthly, the emphasis is on time-series, and the tables and charts contain only a fairly small selection of the economic statistics available. *Social Trends* on the other hand is a substantial annual volume, the 1972 edition consisting of 175 tables, five maps and twenty-seven charts; not all of the charts show changes over time, and the figures themselves are at least as important as their graphical representation.

Each issue starts with four or five fairly lengthy articles, often written by civil service statisticians, and usually signed. The first issue included a general survey of developments in social statistics by Professor Moser and—to give an example of the specialized articles—an article on forecasting housing demand in Great Britain. The 1972 edition broke new ground by the inclusion of a general social commentary, covering the last decade in general but with a longer perspective on subjects such as population.* The commentary had to omit leisure and the environment because of the shortage of data. After the articles comes the main part of the book containing the tables and charts. This consists of twelve sections on the United Kingdom, plus an international section.

Each section is preceded by an introduction describing the tables and commenting on any limitations that may apply to the figures. Some footnotes appear at the bottom of the tables and others in an Appendix towards the end of the book. A second Appendix, of sixteen closely printed pages, is a most useful feature. This partly deals with definitions of technical terms like 'Gini coefficient' and of concepts like 'working population'. It is partly descriptive and informative: for example it summarizes details of the main social security benefits with their rates, dates of introduction and conditions of payment, the arrangements for the raising of the school-leaving age, the system of housing improvement grants, the different types of law-courts and of sentences for offenders. These two Appendices are followed by a comprehensive bibliography, not confined to official sources, and a full alphabetical index. A great merit of *Social Trends* is that it is self-contained: the methodological apparatus is provided, instead of being in a separate supplement, and few users will need to consult other works for more detail. The manner of presentation is also well adapted to making figures intelligible to users with little or no experience of statistics.*

Much use is made of ratios, percentages and index numbers to make the raw figures easier to grasp, and the coloured charts should also prove helpful. The tables and charts can of course be only as good as the original data on which they are based, and on the whole social statistics lag behind economic statistics in this country, for instance with respect to the use of standardized definitions: one can for example find non-standard regions in *Social Trends* and two ways of defining social classes (and market researchers use yet another).

The contents of the tables and charts vary between issues to some extent: a quarter of the

---

* An earlier such commentary written under the auspices of the COI was strongly criticized in an adjournment debate in the Commons [B 73]. Such parliamentary criticism is infrequent; a recent instance was an attack on an *Economic Trends* article in the House of Lords.

* By contrast, the *General Report* [B138] on the Population Census, has ceased to fulfil the function it once served of making the salient results intelligible to the non-specialist user, and has become purely methodological in character.

tables are new in the 1972 edition and sections that have grown particularly since the first issue are those on leisure and the environment. (Some figures on religion might be desirable in a future issue.) Twenty-seven tables that were in the 1971 edition have been dropped; four of these were replaced with charts. A list is provided of tables discontinued from the previous issue, but it might be desirable to make this cumulative for the whole series. Seven tables in the 1972 issue are based on the new *General Household Survey* [QRL 38], and more are promised from this source in future. There is an international section of seventeen tables and one chart which could perhaps be developed further. *Social Trends* is something of a pioneer among British official publications, along with *Facts in Focus* [QRL 33], in having an international section at all, whereas substantial international sections are common in the statistical abstracts of other countries.

Social Trends is to be welcomed not only because it contains a well-chosen collection of figures in its field, but also because it shows by its attractive layout that figures need not be dry as dust. It is particularly valuable for students in the social sciences.

2.2.18   *Trade and Industry*† [QRL 18] was called *The Board of Trade Journal* until October 1970 (and for brevity I shall mostly refer to it anachronistically as 'the Journal' in the remainder of this note). It started under that title as a monthly in 1886, but has been a weekly since January 1900. During the period of the Journal's existence, the scope of its parent Department or group of Departments has varied enormously. It was for example once responsible for labour matters and railways, which have long been with other departments, and has recently regained some subjects—steel and shipping—which were dealt with elsewhere for varying periods. The scope of the Journal has however never wholly coincided with that of the Department; when there was a separate Ministry of Technology many of its statistical series were

published in the Journal, and the figures of levels of food consumption compiled by the Ministry of Agriculture, Fisheries and Food are currently included.

Most of the statistical tables in the Journal belong to regular series and are brought up to date annually, monthly, quarterly or every six months as the case may be. An index in each issue lists all the regular statistical series and the date of the issue in which figures on each subject last appeared. There are also from time to time special articles not in series—for example reporting on 'benchmark' inquiries such as that into credit extended by finance houses or giving the preliminary results of the Census of Distribution. The Journal also sometimes has methodological articles explaining new series and changes in old series or expounding a problem in the compilation of the statistics. Examples of subjects covered in this category are: statistics of retail sales, catering turnover, seasonal adjustment of trade statistics, changes in the weights for the index of wholesale prices, and under-recording of exports.

Each issue has a page of selected indicators on the British economy, almost all on a seasonally adjusted basis. As the Journal is a weekly, it is able to include promptly in this page recent figures which might take two or three weeks to appear in other sources, and which would otherwise have to be sought in press notices or in the newspapers. For example the all-items index of retail prices is available in the Journal some time before it appears in the *Department of Employment Gazette* [QRL 6], *Monthly Digest* [QRL 11] or *Economic Trends* [QRL 9]. The Journal reprints answers to parliamentary questions of interest within the field of the Departments, and they can sometimes be more easily traced through the index to the Journal (which appears quarterly) than through the index to *Hansard* itself. The book reviews and notes on statistical publications are often useful. Certain information, which once appeared in the Journal, has now been 'hived off' to the *Business Monitors*††, for example the detailed tables on overseas transactions. The industrial *Business Monitors*†† are a series of publications each containing the statistics of production or sales of a particular industry or trade; some include other relevant figures, e.g. overseas trade and stocks. They are mostly quarterly though there are a few monthly series; Census of Production Reports now also appear as *Business Monitors*††. In addition to the industrial *Monitors*††, there are publications on some service and distributive trades, and a miscellaneous series, mostly on financial subjects, but also covering cinemas, motor vehicle registrations and tourism. Comprehensive lists of the *Monitors*†† appear in *Trade and Industry* from time to time, and an article explaining the system was published in the issue for 6 September 1973.

The Journal publishes every month the list of release dates of forthcoming economic statistics, which is mentioned in the note on *Economic Trends* [QRL 9] (2.2.9), and also includes the Treasury's monthly article on the economic situation. Starting with the issue for 14 June 1973, there has been a monthly European Communities Commentary, with articles on various aspects of the Community as they affect UK industry and commerce; the commentary includes statistical tables of economic indicators for the countries of the EEC.

Unlike some departments, the Departments of Trade, Industry, and Prices and Consumer Protection make no comprehensive annual report, though they report under statute on certain subjects, e.g. companies, insurance and bankruptcies. The Journal did once include a summary review of the Department's work during the year (in the issue for 27 September 1968), but this has not been repeated. Such a summary would however be very useful.

2.2.19 *The Ulster Year Book*† [QRL 19] first appeared in 1926, and was published at three-year intervals with a break for the war until the issue for 1966–8; annual issues started with that for

1969. The description given here refers to the 1972 edition. The layout resembles that of *Britain —An Official Handbook* [QRL 3] in that it is primarily a textual publication, with figures inserted into the narrative. Besides the figures shown in the text there is a fourteen-page statistical summary at the back giving longer runs of figures than those in the main part of the book. The statistical coverage is in some respects narrower than that of the *Digest of Statistics for Northern Ireland* [QRL 7], and the latter would have to be consulted for example for information on the construction industry, consumers' expenditure, distribution, national income and stocks. The *Digest* would also tend to be more up to date as it appears twice a year. On the other hand the *Year Book* has for example figures of the religious composition of the population for which it might prove a more convenient source than the *Census of Population*††. The *Year Book* has a useful bibliography, which constitutes a select list of the publications of the government of Northern Ireland and includes non-official material as well. There is also a full index.

2.2.20 *Wales—Annual Report* [QRL 20]. See 2.2.8.

Selected Discontinued Serial Publications

2.2.21 *Digest of Scottish Statistics* [QRL 21]. See 2.2.15.

2.2.22 *Economic Surveys* [QRL 22]. These were Command Papers and appeared annually from 1947 to 1962; they were intended to provide economic background for the budget debates in Parliament. At their maximum size they were documents of sixty pages or more containing over thirty tables in a statistical appendix plus others in the text. The tables covered the main subjects of economic interest—national income, balance of payments, production, employment, prices, trade, savings, investment and government finance. There was a general commentary on the UK economy, sometimes with forecasts or plans for the following year, and some issues had notes on individual industries and their exports. The 1959 issue had in an Appendix figures of public investment, which in the following year developed into the separate *Public Investment White Paper* [B 125A]—a very useful series which was however dropped after only four issues. The *Surveys* were succeeded by the *Economic Reports* [QRL 23].

2.2.23 *Economic Reports* [QRL 23]. This series ran for six issues, from the Report on 1962 to that on 1967; the first five appeared as supplements to *Economic Trends* [QRL 9], the last was independent. They were slighter in character than the *Surveys*, with fewer tables (only 10–12 in the statistical appendices), and only one issue dealt with separate industries and did so very briefly. After the cessation of the *Reports*, a few rather lightweight pages of economic comment were (and still are) included in the *Financial Statement and Budget Report*††. (As a result of some parliamentary pressure, this *Report* started to include forecasts of the gross domestic product in 1968.) Apart from these, and the routine monthly article on the UK economy, the Treasury abandoned the task of reporting to Parliament and the public on the economic state of the nation. Three non-governmental sources may be consulted as alternatives: the *National Institute Economic Review* [QRL 12], the *OECD Economic Survey of the United Kingdom* [QRL 14] and *Economic Outlook* [B143], published twice a year by OECD.

2.2.24 *Industry and Employment in Scotland* [QRL 24]. There were seventeen of these annual Command Papers between 1947 and 1963. The earlier issues therefore antedate the *Digest of Scottish Statistics* [QRL 21] and thus form an important source of statistics for that period. Some of them run to over eighty pages and include many tables. They contained general

surveys of the Scottish economy, and material on individual industries. They dealt partly with the past year and partly with the outlook for the future and had both text and tables. The later issues had special sections on industrial building and also incorporated the annual report on Scottish roads. As the roads report is a statutory report, it survived the demise of its parent publication, and was transferred to the *Annual Report of the Scottish Development Department* [B 133]. *Development and Growth in Scotland 1963–64* (Cmnd. 2440) was partially a successor to the earlier series, but no further paper like this appeared. There was therefore a gap with no textual publication on the Scottish economy until the start of the *Scottish Economic Bulletin* [QRL 16] in the summer of 1971.

2.2.25 *London and Cambridge Economic Bulletin* [QRL 25]. See 2.2.4.

2.2.26 *Statistics on Incomes, Prices, Employment and Production* [QRL 26] appeared quarterly between April 1962 and June 1969, running for twenty-nine issues. This publication was connected with prices and incomes policy, of which an earlier manifestation was the *Reports of the Council on Prices, Productivity and Incomes* [B 87]. This Council was set up in 1957 'to keep under review changes in prices, productivity and the level of incomes . . . and to report thereon from time to time'. It was then thought that people's economic behaviour might be modified if enough information was made available, but it eventually became apparent that the publication of statistics was not efficacious in the moderating of wage demands. The Council issued four reports including tables and charts, and one or two methodological pieces may still be found useful, such as notes on the measurement of profit income and the differences between the consumer price index and the index of retail prices. The Council issued no reports after July 1961. The 1962 White Paper *Incomes Policy: The Next Step* (Cmnd. 1626) stated that the government proposed 'to collect together and to publish in convenient form factual information on wage rates, earnings ... and other relevant subjects' which should be borne in mind in wage negotiations and at arbitration. The result was *Statistics on Incomes, Prices, Employment and Production.*

Each issue consisted of about seventy tables arranged in seven parts: general; wages and salaries; company profits, dividends, assets etc.; hours of work; total working population; prices; and production. There were a number of charts and an alphabetical index, and a full technical appendix appeared in every March issue. Some tables did not reappear every time if there were no recent figures available—e.g. those on the dispersion of earnings for which only 1960 figures were available throughout the period. One great advantage of the publication was the long runs, covering fifteen years or more, included in certain of the tables. The series was dropped when it was decided to produce the annual *British Labour Statistics Year Book* [QRL 5].

Books and Non-Serial Publications

2.2.27 *Abstract of British Historical Statistics* [QRL 27] by B. R. Mitchell and P. Deane was first published in 1962, and reprinted with some additional material in 1971. Compilation of this volume must have involved an enormous effort in the assembly of series formerly scattered in many different sources. The aim of the work 'is to provide the user of historical statistics with informed access to a wide range of economic data without the labour of identifying sources or of transforming many annual sources into comparable time series'. The book is arranged in sixteen chapters containing from five to twenty-eight tables; the total number of tables is 194. The subjects of the chapters are: population and vital statistics; the labour force; agriculture; coal; iron and steel; tin, copper and lead; textile industries; transport; building; miscellaneous production

statistics; overseas trade; wages and the standard of living; national income and expenditure; public finance; banking and insurance; and prices. Each chapter starts with a list of tables included, and continues with a commentary on the sources and coverage of the series and on difficulties that may arise in using them. Each table also has notes and references to sources, and the chapters conclude with a bibliography. At the end of the book, there is a general bibliography followed by a subject-index. Explanatory matter is so liberally provided that the work can serve as a guide as well as a statistical source.

The *Abstract* covers only economic statistics, so there is still a similar task waiting to be done for social statistics before the start of Halsey's period in 1900 [QRL 37]. Most series start at some date in the nineteenth century, though some go back to the eighteenth century or earlier. The earliest series—on tin—starts in 1199. The tables finish in 1938, and the territory of the Irish Republic is excluded after 1923. In some countries, for example Sweden, Canada and the United States, volumes of historical statistics are published officially. Here as official publications there have been only the admirable *British Labour Statistics— Historical Abstract 1886–1968* ([QRL 31] see above in 2.2.5) and the *Statistical Digest of the War* [QRL 34]. Users of this volume are grateful to its compilers for filling the gap.

2.2.28 *Second Abstract of British Historical Statistics* [QRL 28] (1971) by B. R. Mitchell and H. G. Jones follows the work just described in approach and layout. It starts in general in 1938, though certain tables not included in the earlier volume go back further. The series mostly finish in 1965 or 1966. The total number of tables is 151. The coverage of the chapters is much the same except that coal has been expanded to include other fuels, other non-ferrous metals have joined tin, copper and lead, and communications have been added to transport. There is however an extra chapter of miscellaneous statistics; this includes some social statistics and the subjects covered are crime, bank-ruptcies, elections and education. Some of these tables start well before the end of the nineteenth century. The introductory commentaries are much shorter than in the main *Abstract*, and include bibliographical material that was given separately in the latter. Less comment was thought to be necessary because of 'the normally greater adequacy of recent statistics'.

2.2.29 *An Analysis of Regional Economic and Social Statistics* by E. Hammond [QRL 29] was published in 1968; there had been an earlier edition in 1965. It tabulates a wide range of figures, generally using index numbers or percentages rather than 'raw' figures, and as far as possible showing figures for each standard region in Great Britain. The selection of figures is 'deliberately orientated towards social affairs', and numerous unofficial sources have been used as well as official ones. It must be the only statistical publication to show as a source for a table the *Good Food Guide* and Egon Ronay's *Guides*.

The sections of the book cover population, employment, housing, education, health, environment and social characteristics. The content of some of these sections is in fact rather wider than one might expect from the headings: 'employment' includes tables on computers and ports, 'environment' includes local government finance, entertainment and transport as well as the previously mentioned tables on recommended eating places. 'Social' includes a variety of tables on, *inter alia*, personal income and expenditure, elections, religion, crime, betting, drunkenness and gipsies. In each table regions are shown in a standard order, with national figures—for Great Britain or England and Wales as a whole—in the middle. Sources are given for each table, and there is a twenty-one-page commentary early in the book bringing out their main points. There is a total of 172 tables, of which thirty-nine are shown in the contents as being 'regional compilations believed not to be available elsewhere'.

Inevitably the book has dated, as it is based on material published up to September 1967, and if a new edition is brought out, it would benefit from an alphabetical subject index.

2.2.30 *Britain in Figures* by Alan F. Sillitoe [QRL 30] has as its subtitle 'A Handbook of Social Statistics'. It consists of graphs, diagrams and charts, each with a commentary on the facing page bringing out the main points and giving any definitions needed to understand the figures fully. The material is arranged in seven parts: population, social data, education, labour, the economy, road transport and mass media and communications. There is a total of sixty-four graphs and diagrams solely on the UK and eleven in which the UK is compared with other countries. The period covered by the time-series varies: 1935 is the preferred starting date unless either the data do not go back as far as that or the subject is one, such as birth rates, where a longer period is desirable. The diagrams include the actual figures as well as their depiction in graphical form but the graphs of time series do not. Some users would need more accurate figures than can be read from the graphs, and the sources for each are given. There is also a brief general bibliography at the back. The book is not intended for the specialist user of statistics who needs precision in his data. Its appeal is primarily to people who like graphs, but the commentaries could be useful to all generalist users of statistics.

A second edition appeared in 1973, updating the statistics that were in the first edition, but broadly following the latter's contents and scope.

2.2.31 *British Labour Statistics: Historical Abstract 1886–1968* [QRL 31]. See 2.2.5.

‡**2.2.32** *British Political Facts 1900–1968* [QRL 32] by D. Butler and J. Freeman has so far appeared in three editions—1963, 1968 and 1969, and a further edition is in preparation. Though, as the name implies, the emphasis is on politics,

this book also contains a considerable selection of general statistics. They are largely drawn from accessible official sources. (The authors call the process of compilation 'systematized plagiarism': this shows great modesty.) To extract the same figures oneself would often be quite time-consuming, so using this book could save much effort. There are also some statistics which the compilers have obtained specially, and others for which the original sources for the earlier years might prove difficult to obtain.

The earlier chapters of the book contain a number of statistical tables on political matters, including elections, the composition of the House of Lords, the creation of peerages, and the size of the civil service analysed by department. There are tables with data that might otherwise be elusive on public opinion polls, sittings of the House of Commons, bills and parliamentary questions and the same applies to the figures later in the book on local elections analysed by party. Chapters IX, X and XI, entitled respectively 'social conditions', 'employment and trade unions' and 'the economy' are largely or entirely statistical. Chapter IX covers, in addition to normal social subjects, demography, migration and transport. The number of series included can of course be only small, given the space available, but the selection looks useful. One reservation is that figures for England and Wales are sometimes given for no particular reason instead of figures for Great Britain or the United Kingdom, and that one or two tables do not specify the areas they refer to. Among the figures later in the book are some on religion, newspaper circulations, and the casualties and cost to Britain of wars and near-wars. Detailed lists of sources are given after each section throughout the book, and there is a general bibliographical note at the end, followed by a subject index.

‡2.2.33 *Facts in Focus* [QRL 33]. This publication is a reasonably priced paperback giving a wide range of statistics. In general its coverage is similar to that of the *Annual Abstract* [QRL 2], but with fewer tables on each subject and showing fewer years. (On leisure and some social subjects it has more figures than the *Abstract*, and unlike the latter it has an international section.) It has 163 tables and thirty-one charts on the UK and eleven international tables. On some subjects, such as crime and education, the tables are necessarily for constituent countries of the UK. Most tables have figures for three dates to cover the decade of the 1960s—1960, 1965 and either 1969 or 1970, according to what figures were available at the date of compilation; but some tables have longer runs, for example those on unemployment, population, industrial disputes and wage indexes. There is no subject index, but it is fairly easy to find what one wants from the list of contents. There is a table of conversion factors, but otherwise little explanatory matter about the figures. However this is probably not needed in a book of this sort, and references are given at the back of the book to sources where more details can be found.

This book corresponds in some ways to the pocket statistical yearbooks which several countries produce annually—for example, East and West Germany, Spain, the Netherlands, Belgium, Poland and New Zealand—but there is no indication as to how frequently it is to appear. It marks a new departure for the Government Statistical Service by being issued jointly with a commercial publisher, thereby gaining wider distribution, and appearing at a much lower price than would have applied if it had been a purely official publication. It should be useful and a further edition was published in 1974.

2.2.34 The *Statistical Digest of the War* [QRL 34] was published in 1951 as part of the UK Civil Series of the official *History of the Second World War* [B 149]—a series comprising twenty-eight volumes. Its aim was 'to bring together the salient facts of the British war effort so far as they are capable of statistical measurement'. The *Digest* is arranged in twelve chapters which cover: population and vital statistics; manpower; social conditions; agriculture and food; fuel and power; raw materials; production; external trade; transport; public finance; national income; and wages and prices. There are twenty-nine pages of notes at the end, included to make the *Digest* as self-contained as possible, and a full subject-index. The arrangement closely resembles that of the *Annual Abstract of Statistics* [QRL 2], but the work is somewhat smaller than the *Abstracts* of the same date. It includes some social statistics but in general naturally concentrates on matters directly connected with the war, so that one will not find in it, for example, figures of beer consumption. The *Annual Abstracts* for the period can be used to supplement it. One omission from it is a list of sources; the introduction refers to war statistics' being 'scattered among many volumes of history and many Command Papers', but unfortunately no references to these are given. This is particularly surprising in view of the inclusion of the volume in a series of histories. On some subjects it is no doubt obvious where one would look further in the individual civil histories on agriculture, coal, financial policy, manpower and so on, but a list of sources, even if only partial, would have been worth including.

2.2.35 *A Statistical Source-Book for Sociologists* [QRL 35] by Graham Sergeant is intended to provide basic information for students of sociology and other courses in general studies. It consists of about 160 tables arranged in ten sections covering: sociological method and population; social diversification; the family; education (the largest section); social mobility; transition from school to work; sociology of politics; work and non-work; sociology of religion; and crime, delinquency and suicide. Each section has a full bibliography, most of the references being to books and articles on sociology rather than to statistical sources. Each of the tables has a note of its source, often with a precise page-reference.

The author has drawn on a large range of non-official books and articles, and this is a valuable feature for those mainly familiar with official statistics. There are a few international comparisons—on divorce and suicide, and on religion with the USA—but almost all the book is concerned with this country. It would benefit from an alphabetical index, as for example a table on public expenditure is rather lost in a section entitled 'work and non-work'. The author hopes to 'revise, update and expand the collection at frequent intervals'.

2.2.36 *A Survey of Social Conditions in England and Wales as illustrated by Statistics* [QRL 36]. See 2.2.37.

2.2.37 *Trends in British Society* [QRL 37] edited by A. H. Halsey has as its subtitle 'a guide to the changing structure of Britain'. It consists of a general introduction and fifteen specialized chapters by different authors. The chapter titles are: population and family; the economic environment; the labour force; social mobility; schools; higher education; electors and elections; urbanization and local government; housing; health; welfare; religion; immigration; crime and penal measures; and leisure. The chapters vary in form but each concludes with statistical tables varying in number from one (social mobility) to fifty-two (health). The text preceding the tables may have the following features (not all are present in every chapter): a description of the statistical sources used, definitions of terms and other notes on the tables, a bibliography or list of sources used for the tables, and a general historical narrative of the evolution of the subject over the period. A general aim of each chapter 'is to guide students in the use of the statistical sources and to point out the dangers in interpreting statistics which are typically collected for administrative purposes rather than to answer questions in the social sciences'. The total number of tables is 382, so this book counts as both a statistical source and a guide to sources and should be very useful in both capacities. There is an index of names only, but full lists of contents and of tables. The coverage of one or two of the chapters is wider than is indicated by their titles: e.g. 'the labour force' includes material on the index of retail prices. The editor envisages bringing out an updated edition when it is needed.

This book covers much of the same ground as an earlier work—Carr-Saunders and others: *A Survey of Social Conditions in England and Wales* [QRL 36]. The latter was confined to England and Wales, whereas Halsey covers Great Britain or the UK, sometimes giving separate figures for Scotland with a few for Northern Ireland and Ireland. Halsey also in general covers a longer period and includes a chapter on elections which Carr-Saunders did not cover. On the other hand, Halsey has nothing on nutrition, to which Carr-Saunders devoted a chapter. The Carr-Saunders book was a new version of a book originally published in 1927, and nutrition was no doubt then very topical. It would be pleasant, but hardly justifiable, to think that the omission of the subject from Halsey meant that the problems had been solved. The earlier versions of the Carr-Saunders book, of which editions appeared in 1927 and 1937, were entitled *A Survey of the Social Structure of England and Wales* [B 112].

Supplement on Recent New Series

‡2.2.38   *The General Household Survey—Introductory Report* [QRL 38] is a most useful new source of social statistics. Surveys have of course long been employed by government statisticians, but hitherto on separate subjects, for example family expenditure. The General Household Survey differs by being concerned with several subjects, and thus meeting some of the research needs of different government departments simultaneously. This *Report* covers population, housing, employment, education and health, and on these topics one aim of the Survey has been to supply information not available from existing official statistics.

The Survey is a continuing activity and the subjects covered will vary over time in accordance with departmental needs. This note is concerned with the first, and so far only, published *Report*.

The *Report* is a very reasonably priced volume of 570 pages consisting of chapters on each of the five subjects mentioned, preceded by three introductory methodological chapters, and followed by a further chapter on organization and full specimens of the forms used, interviewers' instructions and so on. All told, the supporting material takes up almost two-fifths of the book, but probably much of this needs to be given only once in such detail and will not have to be repeated in future reports. In the data chapters, the total number of tables is 192, with many illustrative diagrams in addition; the chapter on housing is the longest with over one-third of the tables. The following is a selection only of some of the subjects dealt with, chosen to illustrate the range of material included: family intentions (eventual size of family expected at marriage and later); the coloured population, both as a subject in itself and in relation to housing; moving house; job satisfaction; reasons for absence from work; sick pay arrangements for employees; private study for educational qualifications; multiple jobs; visits to doctors. To some extent the Survey brings up to date earlier work by the Government Social Survey, but on other subjects it breaks fresh ground. Where possible, there are comparisons between the Survey and other sources—e.g. the *Population Census*††, the *Family Expenditure Survey*†† and the National *House Condition Survey* [B 150]—and where discrepancies are found, explanations are sought. The *Report* contains only a selection of the total data which could be derived from the Survey; well over a thousand tables on the year 1971 were originally compiled.

Future similar multi-subject reports are promised as well as reports on selected topics. Some results may also appear in other government publications, and indeed *Social Trends* [QRL 17] was the first place in which any of the data were made available. The *Report* lists examples of further work being undertaken: housing costs; high-rise dwellings; training opportunities in jobs; weekend working; smoking habits; hospital waiting lists. The somewhat miscellaneous nature of this list emphasizes the need for a general index to the contents of statistical sources, because it is only through the inclusion of the Survey in such an index that its full exploitation by users can be ensured. It would be a great pity if users outside government failed to avail themselves of the data because of ignorance of its existence.

‡2.2.39　*Local Government Trends* [QRL 39] is produced by the Chartered Institute of Public Finance and Accountancy (CIPFA) (formerly the Institute of Municipal Treasurers and Accountants). The first issue, for 1973, is a book of 300 pages, containing in total some 340 tables, charts, graphs and maps. It was produced by a co-operative effort of over forty contributors, plus members of the Institute's staff. Its aim is to help remedy two shortcomings in the field of local government statistics: the lack of a general work of reference which assembles the main indicators of local government activity; and the need for improved information to help local government in its planning processes and in its dialogue with the central government. The authors recognize that their volume goes only some of the way to fulfilling these aims, because of the deficiencies in the basic information in some of the fields they cover.

There are twelve chapters consisting roughly of equal proportions of statistics and text. Many of the tables are reprinted from other sources, so users who already have access to the latter are likely to find that the book makes a fresh contribution mainly in the text portions. The Institute however feels that bringing the data together makes possible the identification of gaps in current statistics. Certainly the book draws on a wide variety of sources, some of which would probably be overlooked by users. The sources include not only standard statistical reference works but also,

for example, a Report of a House of Lords Select Committee, answers to parliamentary questions and the Civic Trust (for figures on conservation areas).

A list follows of the titles of the chapters, with notes on some of the special subjects covered: government influences, a chapter relating to the pattern of local government before reorganization and to the initial impact of reorganization; social conditions, with special treatment of the Urban Aid Programme and the General Household Survey; economic conditions, as they affect the resources available to central government, with inflation as the special topic; education, including a feature on the under-fives; environmental health, with sections on refuse collection and disposal, noise and air pollution; housing; leisure; personal social services; public protection—the shortest chapter, covering consumer protection, fire services and the police; transportation, with a note on transportation grants; development, covering distribution (with a special note on hypermarkets), construction, investment and planning; and lastly administration, including tables on local government manpower and the central purchasing of supplies. It is intended to update annually a core of information in each chapter, and vary the special topics from issue to issue. This is much the same system as that used in *Social Trends* [QRL 17], and in both cases it is satisfactory as long as there is a proper arrangement for the indexing of previous special topics such as that used in the *Commentary* volume of the *Registrar General's Statistical Review for England and Wales* [B 162].

Inevitably the quality of different parts of the book varies; in a quick survey of the contents, useful historical articles on housing and personal social services catch the eye, as does a technical note on the measurement of noise. On the other hand the table on public investment in sports facilities is derived from a paper in a series dropped by the Treasury in 1963 (it is, of course, not the Institute's fault that these are the latest published figures), and the table on the consumption of various fuels could well have more recent figures than for 1969 and need not have come from such a secondary source. International comparisons are given on inflation, hours of work, paid holidays and house completions, and it is not immediately obvious why they are provided only for these topics, if they are to be given at all. The book badly needs an alphabetical index; one would not know from either the list of chapter titles or that of tables that the book contains material on transportation grants and flexible working hours in local government—both of which subjects are dealt with only in the text portions of the book and are therefore not listed. The Institute hopes to refine and improve *Local Government Trends* in future issues, and use it to fill gaps currently existing in the available statistics. There is every sign that it should be a useful publication.

2.2.40 *Welsh Economic Trends* [QRL 40] first appeared in 1974; there is no indication of its planned frequency. It is a booklet of forty pages containing fifty tables, plus some maps and diagrams, arranged in ten subject groups. These are: population, regional income and expenditure, employment, unemployment, earnings and hours, household income and expenditure, consumers' expenditure, output, capital expenditure and public expenditure. There are also appendices on the census of employment and on detailed employment and unemployment figures for individual areas in Wales. Comparisons are given in some tables with the UK or with Great Britain and with other standard regions. Brief remarks are appended to the tables to bring out their main points. The publication seems to contain a well-chosen selection of figures on the Welsh economy.

3 Needs and Desirable Improvements in the Field Surveyed

3.1 Government Publications Generally

The difficulties of the present system of categories of government publications and their indexes were described in Chapter 1 of this review. It should not be impossible to devise a more rational system of categories than the present one, and on the whole the best thing might be to merge them. Under current arrangements, it can need considerable detective work to discover if a series has been switched to another category or has succumbed to the rather high rate of mortality to which statistical publications are subject. Nobody would I think claim that parliamentary publications were inherently more important than non-parliamentary ones: the 1921 definition (see 1.3.1 *supra*) has long ceased to apply, and Treasury guidance given in 1958 was extremely vague on the distinction between the two categories ([B 81], p. 9). Publication of a document as a House of Commons paper can give ministers and officials protection against suits for libel ([B 90], pp. 37–8), but there would otherwise appear to be little distinction between the two groups. There seems to be even less justification for direct selling of publications by departments when there is a central organization for this purpose (HMSO). Besides making it difficult for users to trace publications, the transfer of publishing responsibility from HMSO can also result in a steep rise in the price. For example, a set of *Civil Aviation Business Monitors* [B 120] used to cost £5 p.a., whereas *CAA Monthly Statistics*†† published by the Civil Aviation Authority cost £25 plus an additional sum for the Annual Statistics. On the other hand, the sharing of a publication with a commercial publisher, as with *Facts in Focus* [QRL 33] (2.2.33) may result in a lower price than if HMSO were the sole publisher.

The following changes appear to be needed to eliminate the worst inconveniences of the present system:

1. The inclusion of parliamentary papers in HMSO sectional lists. These are the nearest that HMSO comes to publishing a subject guide, and it seems absurd to exclude perhaps the key document on a subject because it happens to be a parliamentary paper.
2. The inclusion in all HMSO catalogues (with the possible exception of the daily list) of publications issued directly by departments. This would make it possible to trace items that are now virtually untraceable.
3. The tidying-up of the current confused situation on the publications of the nationalized industries and other public bodies (described in 1.3.1).

The next need is for the decline of the annual report to be arrested and reversed. As Sir Arthur Cockfield has said, 'there is a strong and possibly unanswerable case for the publication of statistical information which is produced as part of the efficient functioning of a [Government] Department' ([B 44], p. 527). The desirable situation would be for each public corporation and most government departments to publish an informative, substantial annual report with plenty of statistics; this is far from being realized at present, and the situation is deteriorating. The public are after all indirectly the owners of public corporations and the source of funds for departments, and it would be appropriate for both types of organization to report fully on their activities. The current orthodox view is that in all spheres a continually increasing amount of information is being published, and a text cited for this comfortable assertion comes from the Report of the Fulton Committee [B 63], p. 91: 'We welcome the increasing provision of the detailed information on which decisions are made.'[1] The Report added that it should be carried much further, and that 'it is healthy for a democracy increasingly to press to be consulted and informed'. From the context of this statement, however, it is clear that the committee was not thinking of the flow of information in general, but only of that connected with specific decisions—and a good example is the enormous documentation of the inquiry into the Third London Airport.[2] As far as statistics are concerned, I have given several examples in this review of areas in which the amount published has been reduced, and the task of the seeker of information made more difficult.

One field in which there has been a marked decline in the amount published is official material on the general course of the economy. The story of the *Economic Surveys* [QRL 22] and *Economic Reports* [QRL 23] has been told earlier (2.2.22 and 2.2.23), and the pattern with plans is similar. There were five economic planning documents between 1963 and 1970, but there has been none since.[3] The first two were issued by NEDO (in 1963 and 1964), but the third—the *National Plan* [QRL 42] was ‡issued by the government itself. The two remaining papers, both green (the colour indicating a

reduced degree of commitment to them on the part of the government), were progressively slighter. A monthly economic commentary at first looked a promising development. This started in January 1967 and was originally carried by *Economic Trends* [QRL 9] (see 2.2.9). By early 1974 the article was down to only two pages, except for the March issue. The latter reproduces the text of the economic review from the *Financial Statement and Budget Report*††—a vestigial survival of the old *Economic Surveys* [QRL 22]. These reviews do however include the short-term economic forecasts (which sometimes do not look very far ahead), the publication of which was conceded as a result of pressure from MPs in 1967. Thus in the field of official economic comment and associated figures, the user now has only the annual brief piece in the *Financial Statement*†† and the somewhat shrunken monthly article, which is less widely circulated than formerly because it has been dropped from *Economic Trends*. There are, of course, commentaries in the *Bank of England Quarterly Bulletin*††, as well as those mentioned earlier in the notes on the *National Institute Economic Review* [QRL 12] (2.2.12) and on the *OECD Economic Survey of the UK* [QRL 14] (2.2.14), but there does seem to be a need for a greater flow of material from the government itself in this field.

By comparison a minor need, but one which could save much time, is for announcements about publications that are discontinued or abandoned, such as the two volumes of *Commentaries* on the 1961 *Census of Population*††. Sometimes the last issue of a series informs the reader of its discontinuance; more often, like *Protective Duties* [B 125] or the *Public Investment White Paper* [B 125A], they simply dry up without notice.* One is never quite sure when to give up hope of long overdue works, as publications can come out very late, for example the *Supplement to*

---

[1] However, some years later a member of the Committee—Lord Crowther-Hunt—wrote that 'it is not in the nature of governments and their bureaucracies to provide the people with more information than constitutional and other pressures can prise out of them' ([B 107], p. 35). In fairness I think one should add that this statement could not in general currently be said to apply to statistics in this country.

[2] Another field in which there has been a recent expansion of information is research and development. As a result of a recommendation of the Select Committee on Science and Technology ([B 106], para. 177), some departments are now publishing annual reports on their research activities. Five departments have produced reports so far (1974), of which four were published by HMSO; the remaining department chose to publish the report itself, thus reducing its circulation.

[3] A much earlier paper of 1948, *Memoranda submitted to the OEEC relating to Economic Affairs in the period 1949 to 1953*, Cmd. 7572, could be regarded as the UK's first 'Four Year Plan'.

* One would have had to consult an Act of Parliament to ‡know that there was going to be no *Quinquennial Review of the National Insurance Scheme* for 1964–8.

the 1961 *Census of Distribution* [B 163] which appeared in 1972. Perhaps announcements on these matters could appear in *Statistical News* [B 14].

Publications move between categories, as has been described, and users have to try to keep track of them. In the same way, tables move between publications, and similarly users have to try to remain informed. A few examples may make the point. As mentioned in 1.3.1, tables formerly in *Road Motor Vehicles* [B 127] (Ministry of Transport) turned up in *The Motor Industry of Great Britain* (SMMT) [B 156]. The surveys of local authority loan debt have sometimes appeared in *Economic Trends* [QRL 9] and sometimes in *Financial Statistics*††, and several tables formerly in the *Memorandum on the Estimates*†† were transferred in 1974 to other sources. Failure to keep abreast of transfers can lead to misunderstandings: the late Harold Wincott once based part of an article on the supposition that the figures of the national debt had been suppressed because they were so unfavourable, when in fact all that had happened was that the figures had been transferred from the *Financial Statement*†† to *Financial Statistics*††. Where such transfers are unavoidable—and it would obviously be desirable for them to be kept to the minimum—it would help users if an announcement could appear prominently in the publication originally carrying the transferred material.

One need in the field of book production may be mentioned. Official statistical publications are mostly well printed, but it should be realized that glueing pages down one edge is not a satisfactory method of assembling reference works (though it may be suitable for pulp fiction). Some of the publications mentioned in this review are intensively used in libraries and elsewhere, and for a book costing £3 or more to disintegrate the first time it is opened is hardly satisfactory.

A final need under this heading is for a greatly improved index to *Hansard*. Much time and effort must be spent throughout the public service in the compilation of private indexes, because of the defects of the official one. It is hardly possible for somebody with access only to the official index to exploit fully the richness as a statistical source of answers to parliamentary questions.

3.2 Guides

The paramount need is for the *Guide to Current Official Statistics* now being prepared by the CSO. This will *list* statistics, but descriptions are also required. The series of reviews including the present one will eventually cover much ground, but there is a need for official works as well. New editions would be welcome of the series *Guides to Official Sources* [B 1, 9–13], as would further publications dealing with subjects not so far covered. (These guides appeared mostly in the 1950s and only one has been fairly recently updated.) A new edition is also needed of *Government Statistical Services* [B 68] which is now over ten years old. This was a slim pamphlet and much less detailed than the equivalent foreign publications; to take two examples, *Statistical Services of the US Government* (1968 ed.) [B 166] is a book of over 150 pages, and *A Survey of German Federal Statistics* (1971) [B 169] is, at 120 pages, only an abridgement of the full version in German.

3.3 General Sources

One apparent gap in British general sources is a weekly publication like those produced by the USA and Canada. I doubt however if there is a real need for one, as *Trade and Industry* [QRL 18] appears weekly with a page of leading indicators; the *Financial Times* and *Economist* also carry summary tables; and the monthly list of publication dates of press notices in *Economic Trends* [QRL 9] and *Trade and Industry* quickly takes the user to the right issue of the newspapers, or to press notices if he has access to them. A greater need is probably for a cheap and expendable monthly, such as the US *Current Economic Indicators* [B 141]. *Economic Trends* originally fulfilled this role, costing 2/– (10p) when it first appeared in November 1953, but has over the years become increasingly elaborate and expensive, and now at 85p per issue caters for a different market. (But changes are currently—in 1974—planned in its character.) *Facts in Focus* [QRL 33], if it became a regular publication, could similarly be a cheap and widely distributed annual or biennial.

Comments on the contents of individual publications have been made earlier, and I should like to add only one general comment here—that because of the departmental basis on which most statistics are collected, subjects can be neglected if they traverse departmental boundaries. To take two examples: the Estimates Committee ([B 69], para 91) commented on the paucity of the information on salaries, and the situation has not greatly changed since the Committee wrote. There is however a large amount of information on salaries in the public sector, which includes much of the salaried population, but this information is scattered over several different departments. On wage earners there is an annual fat volume— *Time Rates of Wages and Hours of Work* [B 170]— and there would appear to be a place for at least a summary table on salaries. It could start with specimen scales for different grades of say hospital doctors, nurses, judges, the armed forces, school and university teachers, local authority staff and

the civil service, and perhaps grow if more information became available.★

The second example relates to means tests. A topic arousing great interest for some time now is the impact on the finances of families as gross earnings rise, of the resulting changes in income tax and national insurance contributions and in means-tested benefits, such as family income supplement, free school meals, rate and rent rebates, remission of national health service charges and so on. Requests for official figures used to receive the answer that no one department is responsible, and in the end it needed a request ‡from a Select Committee to result in the publication of the required statistics ([B 109], pp. 49–51 and 426–9). In this instance, as with the economic forecasts and the departmental research reports, pressure from a Committee or group of MPs was efficacious in securing publication where a single Member might have had less influence.

3.4 Conclusion

Statistical users in the UK have access to a range of general publications that on the whole are well adapted to their needs. In the fields of guides, indexes and publishing arrangements for statistical publications generally, some changes and improvements are desirable.

★ The pre-war *Statistical Abstracts* had figures of average salaries in school and university teaching.

Quick Reference List of
General Statistical Sources

QUICK REFERENCE LIST OF GENERAL STATISTICAL SOURCES

Notes: A=Annual; M=Monthly; Q=Quarterly; W=Weekly

If there is no detailed note on a source in Chapter 2, any reference to it is shown in the 'main text reference' column.
Bibliographies are not mentioned if they are fairly brief.
All government publications are non-parliamentary unless otherwise stated.
The dates shown for first and last issues are generally those on the cover, which may not always be the same as the date of publication.
Details of earlier titles and earlier departments responsible will be found in the text.

CURRENT REGULAR SERIAL PUBLICATIONS

Serial No.	Organization responsible	Title	Date of first issue	Frequency	Publisher	Bibl.	Incl. in Table I	Price and remarks	Main text ref.
[QRL 1]	Central Statistical Office	Abstract of Regional Statistics	1965	A	HMSO, London	Yes	Yes	£2·70	2.2.1
[QRL 2]	Central Statistical Office	Annual Abstract of Statistics	1854	A	HMSO, London	Yes	Yes	£4·00	2.2.2
[QRL 3]	Central Office of Information	Britain—An Official Handbook	1954(b)	A	HMSO, London	Yes	No	£3·15	2.2.3
[QRL 4]	London and Cambridge Economic Service	British Economy—Key Statistics	1963(c)	Every two years(a)	Times Newspapers Ltd	Yes	Yes	Out of print	2.2.4
[QRL 5]	Department of Employment	British Labour Statistics Yearbook	1969	A	HMSO, London	No	Yes	£12·00	2.2.5
[QRL 6]	Department of Employment	Department of Employment Gazette	1893	M	HMSO, London	No	Yes	90p £12·12 p.a.	2.2.6
[QRL 7]	Ministry of Finance, Northern Ireland	Digest of Statistics, Northern Ireland	March 1954	Twice yearly	HMSO, Belfast	No	Yes	£1·50	2.2.7
[QRL 8]	Welsh Office	Digest of Welsh Statistics	1954	A	HMSO, Cardiff	No	Yes	£2·50	2.2.8
[QRL 9]	Central Statistical Office	Economic Trends	Nov. 1953	M	HMSO, London	Yes	Yes	£1·15 £16·64 p.a. including Supplement	2.2.9
[QRL 10]	HMSO	London Gazette	1665	4 times weekly	HMSO, London	No	No	10p £28·58 p.a.	2.2.10
[QRL 11]	Central Statistical Office	Monthly Digest of Statistics	Jan. 1946	M	HMSO, London	No	Yes	£1·20 £16·38 p.a. including Supplement	2.2.11
[QRL 11A]	Central Statistical Office	Monthly Digest of Statistics—Definitions Supplement	Jan. 1946	A	HMSO, London	Yes	No	55p. Published at the same time as Jan. issue of Monthly Digest	2.2.11
[QRL 12]	National Institute of Economic and Social Research	National Institute Economic Review	Jan. 1959	Q	National Inst. of Econ. and Soc. Research	No	Yes	£1·75, £6 p.a.	2.2.12

Serial No.	Organization responsible	Title	Date of first issue	Frequency	Publisher				Main text ref.
[QRL 13]	Ministry of Finance, Northern Ireland	Northern Ireland Economic Report	1964	A (d)	HMSO, Belfast	No	No	52p. Succeeded Northern Ireland Economic Survey —only one issue, May 1953, NI Cmd. 446	2.2.13
[QRL 14]	Organization for Economic Co-operation and Development	OECD Economic Survey—the United Kingdom	1953	A	OECD, but also obtainable from HMSO	No	No	70p	2.2.14
[QRL 15]	Scottish Office	Scottish Abstract of Statistics	1971	A	HMSO, Edinburgh	No	Yes	£2·40	2.2.15
[QRL 16]	Scottish Office	Scottish Economic Bulletin	1971	Twice yearly	HMSO, Edinburgh	No	Yes	90p	2.2.16
[QRL 17]	Central Statistical Office	Social Trends	1970	A	HMSO, London	Yes	Yes	£3·30	2.2.17
[QRL 18]	Departments of Trade, Industry, Prices and Consumer Protection	Trade and Industry	1886	W	HMSO, London	No	Yes	20p £15·34 p.a.	2.2.18
[QRL 19]	Northern Ireland Information Service	Ulster Yearbook	1926	A	HMSO, Belfast	Yes	Yes	£2	2.2.19
[QRL 20]	Welsh Office	Wales—Annual Report	1945-6	A (d)	HMSO, Cardiff	No	No	79p. Command Paper. No longer contains many statistics.	2.2.8

SELECTED DISCONTINUED SERIAL PUBLICATIONS

Serial No.	Organization responsible	Title	Date of first issue	Date of last issue	Frequency	Publisher	Remarks	Main text ref.
[QRL 21]	Scottish Office	Digest of Scottish Statistics	April 1953	April 1971	Twice yearly	HMSO, Edinburgh	Succeeded by [QRL 15 and 16].	2.2.15
[QRL 22]	Treasury	Economic Survey	1947	1962	A	HMSO, London	Command Papers; succeeded by [QRL 23]	2.2.22
[QRL 23]	Treasury	Economic Report	1962	1967	A	HMSO, London	Command Papers	2.2.23
[QRL 24]	Scottish Development Department	Industry and Employment in Scotland	1946	1962-3	A	HMSO, Edinburgh	Command Papers	2.2.24
[QRL 25]	London and Cambridge Economic Service	London and Cambridge Economic Bulletin	1923	Dec. 1965	Q	Times Newspapers Ltd	Published 1952-65 in the Times Review of Industry/Industry and Technology. Subsequent issues in The Times, but without regular statistical tables.	2.2.4
[QRL 26]	Department of Employment and Productivity	Statistics on Incomes, Prices, Employment and Production	April 1962	June 1969	Q	HMSO, London		2.2.26

BOOKS AND NON-SERIAL PUBLICATIONS

Serial No.	Author	Title	Date of most recent edition	Publisher	Bibl.	Price and remarks	Main text ref.
[QRL 27]	B. R. Mitchell and P. Deane	Abstract of British Historical Statistics	1971	CUP	Yes	£4·50	2.2.27
[QRL 28]	B. R. Mitchell and H. G. Jones	Second Abstract of British Historical Statistics	1971	CUP	No	£3·40 Sequel to [QRL 27]	2.2.28
[QRL 29]	E. Hammond	An Analysis of Regional Economic and Social Statistics	1968	University of Durham, Rowntree Research Unit	No	£1·25	2.2.29
[QRL 30]	A. F. Sillitoe	Britain in Figures	1973	Penguin Books	No	£1·00	2.2.30
[QRL 31]	Department of Employment	British Labour Statistics—Historical Abstract 1886–1968	1971	HMSO, London	No	£7·00	2.2.5
[QRL 32]	D. Butler and J. Freeman	British Political Facts 1900–1968	1969(e)	Macmillan	Yes	£3·50	2.2.32
[QRL 33]	Central Statistical Office	Facts in Focus	1974	Penguin Books, in association with HMSO	No	60p	2.2.33
[QRL 34]	Central Statistical Office	Statistical Digest of the War	1951	HMSO & Longmans	No	Out of print	2.2.34
[QRL 35]	G. Sergeant	Statistical Source Book for Sociologists	1972	Macmillan	Yes	75p	2.2.35
[QRL 36]	Sir A. Carr-Saunders, D. Caradog Jones and C. A. Moser	A Survey of Social Conditions in England and Wales as illustrated by Statistics	1958	OUP	Yes	£1·50. Succeeds A Survey of the Social Structure of England and Wales.	2.2.37
[QRL 37]	A. H. Halsey (ed.)	Trends in British Society since 1900	1972	Macmillan	Yes	£4·95	2.2.37

RECENT NEW SERIES

Serial No.	Author	Title	Date of most recent issue	Publisher	Price and remarks	Main text ref.
[QRL 38]	Office of Population Censuses, Social Survey Division	General Household Survey—Introductory Report	1973 (e)	HMSO, London	£1·80	2.2.38
[QRL 39]	Chartered Institute of Public Finance and Accountancy	Local Government Trends	1974 (e)	CIPFA, London	£2·50. To be annual	2.2.39
[QRL 40]	Welsh Office	Welsh Economic Trends	1975	HMSO, Cardiff	£2	2.2.40

GOVERNMENT ECONOMIC PLANNING DOCUMENTS ETC.
(none have detailed notes in Chapter 2)

[QRL 41]	K. S. Isles and N. Cuthbert	*An Economic Survey of Northern Ireland*	1957	HMSO, Belfast	£1·75p. Statistical appendix of fifty-two tables and many others in the text	2.2.13
[QRL 42]	Department of Economic Affairs	*The National Plan* (Cmnd. 2764)	1965	HMSO, London	£1·50. Previous and subsequent papers are not listed as their statistical content does not justify counting them as general sources.	3.1
[QRL 43]	Sir Robert Hall and others	*Report of The Joint Working Party on the Economy of Northern Ireland* (NI Cmd. 446)	1963	HMSO, Belfast	27½p. Statistical appendix of thirty-four tables and others in the text	2.2.13
[QRL 44]	Scottish Office	*The Scottish Economy 1965 to 1970. A Plan for Expansion* (Cmnd. 2864)	1966	HMSO, Edinburgh	62½p	
[QRL 45]	G. L. Rees and others	*Survey of the Welsh Economy*	1973	HMSO, London	£1·20. Research Paper No. 8 of the Commission on the Constitution. Statistical appendix of fifty-four tables plus sixty-four tables in the text	
[QRL 46]	Welsh Office	*Wales—The Way Ahead* (Cmnd. 3334)	1967	HMSO, Cardiff	67½p	

(a) no issue for 1900–68
(b) date of first issue put on sale
(c) on 1900–62
(d) discontinued after 1973 ed., see Addenda
(e) see Addenda

General Bibliography

This consists of five sections:

1. Guides, commentaries, etc.—official: listed alphabetically by title.
2. Guides, commentaries, etc.—unofficial: listed alphabetically by author.
3. Other works, with a named person as author: listed alphabetically by author.
4. Other works, without a named person as author: listed alphabetically by title.
5. Supplement of additional references. This consists of two sections: 5(a) consists of late entries to the first four sections of the bibliography which could not be inserted into their correct positions without a complete renumbering of all the references. 5(b) contains titles of statistical publications which were mentioned in the text as examples. It was decided only at a late stage to cite these fully.

The numbering is continuous throughout. All publications designated HC (House of Commons Papers) and Cmd. or Cmnd. (Command Papers) are published by HMSO (Her Majesty's Stationery Office), so the letters HMSO are not included in the references for these items. Where HMSO is mentioned the items are non-parliamentary papers (for the distinction, see above, 1.3.1). The place of publication of all items is London unless otherwise stated. The styles of address of authors shown are those possessed at the time at which they wrote. Annotations are given to some titles where they are thought to be helpful.

1 GUIDES, COMMENTARIES, ETC.—OFFICIAL

In addition to the titles listed, *Economic Trends* and *Statistical News* contain articles surveying the statistics on separate subjects.

All items in this section are published by HMSO as non-parliamentary papers unless otherwise stated.

[B 1] *Agricultural and Food Statistics—a Guide to Official Sources.* Ministry of Agriculture, Fisheries and Food, 3rd ed. 1974. Studies in official statistics, No. 23. Successor to *Guide to Official Sources*, No. 4; see [B 9]–[B 13], below.

[B 2] *Directory of Construction Statistics.* Ministry of Public Building and Works, 1968. See also [B 14].

[B 3] *Distributive Trades Statistics—a Guide to Official Sources.* NEDO, 1970.

[B 4] *Education Statistics for the United Kingdom.* Produced jointly by the education departments. This contains a note on sources of UK education statistics, for example on pages xiv–xviii of the 1970 edition.

[B 5] *Electronics Industry Statistics and their Sources.* NEDO, 1968. Published by NEDO.

[B 6] *Food Statistics—a Guide to Major Official and Unofficial UK Sources.* NEDO, 1969. Published by NEDO.

[B 7] *Guide to Current Official Statistics.* Permanent Consultative Committee on Official Statistics. Annual issues from 1922 (pub. 1923) to 1938 (pub. 1939).

[B 8] *Guide to Statistics Collected by HM Factory Inspectorate.* Ministry of Labour, 1960.

Guides to Official Sources. Interdepartmental Committee on Social and Economic Research.

[B 9] No. 1 *Labour Statistics*, third ed., 1958 (updated in *Ministry of Labour Gazette*, Sep. 1961, p. 381).,

[B 10] No. 2 *Census Reports of Great Britain 1801–1931*, 1951.

[B 11] No. 3 *Local Government Statistics*, 1953. (No. 4 replaced by [B 1], above.)

[B 12] No. 5 *Social Security Statistics*, 1961.

[B 13] No. 6 *Census of Production Reports*, 1961.

[B 14] *Inventory of Construction Statistics.* 3 vols., Ministry of Public Building and Works, 1968. Not published for general sale, but available for consultation at certain libraries. See also item [B 2].

[B 15] *List of Principal Statistical Series and Publications.* CSO, 2nd ed, 1974. Studies in official statistics, No. 20. Amendments to this publication are published in *Statistical News.* Successor to [B 16].

[B 16] *List of Principal Statistical Series Available—Economic, Financial and Regional Statistics.* CSO, 1965. Studies in official statistics, No. 11. Replaced by [B 15].

[B 17] *National Accounts Statistics—Sources and Methods.* CSO, 2nd ed., 1968. Edited by R. Maurice. Studies in official statistics, No. 13. This work is brought up to date by the notes at the back of the latest annual edition of *National Income and Expenditure* (The Blue Book).

New Contributions to Economic Statistics—collections of articles reprinted from *Economic Trends:*

[B 18] 1st series, 1957–8 Studies in official statistics, No. 5

[B 19] 2nd series, 1959–61 Studies in official statistics, No. 9.

[B 20] 3rd series Feb. 1962–Feb. 1964 Studies in official statistics, No. 10.

[B 21] 4th series Aug. 1964–Aug. 1966 Studies in official statistics, No. 12.

[B 22] 5th series, May 1967–May 1969 Studies in official statistics, No. 15.

[B 23] 6th series, Nov. 1969–Nov. 1971 Studies in official statistics, No. 19.

[B 24] *Statistical News—Developments in British Official Statistics.* CSO, quarterly, May 1968–

[B 25] *Strategic Plan for the South East—Studies Vol. 4.* Dept. of the Environment, 1971, pp. 228–33. Regional Statistics—based on a report by the Standing Conference on London and South East Regional Planning. (Also included in *Greater London Research—Quarterly Bulletin of the Research and Intelligence Unit of the GLC,* Dec. 1969, No. 9, p. 20.)

2   GUIDES, COMMENTARIES ETC.—UNOFFICIAL

[B 26] Barker, W. *Local Government Statistics*, Institute of Municipal Treasurers, 1965.

[B 27] Blyth, C. *The Use of Economic Statistics*, Allen & Unwin, 1960. Twelve chapters, each dealing with a problem in applied economics and explaining the statistical sources needed. At the back a reference table of UK economic statistics.

[B 28] Burrington, G. *How to find out about Statistics*, Pergamon, Oxford, 1972.

[B 29] Carter, C. F. and Roy, A. D. *British economic statistics—a report*, Cambridge University Press, 1954. (National Institute of Economic and Social Research—Economic and Social Studies XIV.) A critical review of published statistics, both in general and in six special fields. Some of the recommendations are still valid. There is a full bibliography and reference table of principal British economic statistics with their sources.

[B 30] Connor, L. R. and Morrell, A. J. H. *Statistics in Theory and Practice*, Pitman, 6th ed., 1972. The last eight chapters are on sources of statistics.

[B 31] Devons, E. *An Introduction to British Economic Statistics*, Cambridge University Press, 1955. Still useful in spite of the date of publication.

[B 32] Edwards, B. *Sources of Economic and Business Statistics*, Heinemann, 1972. (A companion volume on social statistics is in preparation.) [B113]

[B 33] Fletcher, J. *The Use of Economics Literature*, Butterworth, 1971. Chapter 10 deals with economic statistics, and Chapter 7 with British government publications.

[B 34] Harvey, J. M. *Sources of Statistics*, Bingley, 2nd ed., 1971. One chapter on general sources, and thirteen chapters on statistical sources in different fields.

[B 35] Hays, S. *An Outline of Statistics*, Longmans, 8th ed., 1970. Chapters 13–20 are on sources.

[B 36] Ilersic, A. R. *Statistics*, H. F. L. (Publishers), 13th ed., 1964. Three chapters respectively on social, vital and economic statistics and sources for them. References to sources are given for most sections of the chapters.

[B 37] Kendall, M. G. (ed.) *The Sources and Nature of the Statistics of the United Kingdom.* 2 vols. Oliver and Boyd, vol. 1, 1952, vol. 2, 1957. Reprints of articles on statistics in certain fields from the JRSS. There are twenty articles in vol. 1, nineteen in vol. 2.

[B 38] Lewes, F. M. M. *Statistics of the British Economy*, Allen & Unwin, 1967. Eight chapters on specific topics plus an introduction. Each chapter has a bibliography listing sources and commentaries.

[B 39] Marris, R. *Economic Arithmetic*, 1958. Chapter 2 deals with sources of economic statistics in the UK.

[B 40] Moser, C. and Kalton, G. *Survey Methods in Social Investigation*, Heinemann Educational Books, 2nd ed., 1971. Chapter 1 contains a useful account of selected surveys, both government and private, and gives references to reports on them.

[B 41] Nicholson, R. J. *Economic Statistics and Economic Problems*, McGraw-Hill, 1969. Ten chapters in each of which statistics are used to investigate specific economic problems. Full bibliographies to each chapter.

[B 42] Pemberton, J. E. *British Official Publications*, Pergamon, Oxford, 1971. Chapter 15 deals with statistics. Various other chapters are helpful on official publications generally.

[B 43] Wills, G. (ed.) *Sources of UK Marketing Information*, Nelson, 1969. Two main sections of the book, on prime sources and the marketing environment, deal with statistics of general interest and the others will also be found useful on special topics. There are indexes of products/services/industries and of titles of sources.

3   OTHER WORKS, WITH NAMED PERSON AS AUTHOR

[B 44] Allen, Sir Roy. 'On official statistics and official statisticians', *JRSS*, 1970, **133**, 509.

[B 45] Berman, L. S. 'Recent improvements in official economic statistics', *JRSS*, 1971, **134**, 630.

[B 46] Bridges, Lord, *The Treasury*, Allen & Unwin, 2nd ed., 1966. New Whitehall Series.

[B 47] Burch, R. F. 'Statistical surveys conducted by the National Board for Prices and Incomes', *Statistical News*, 1971, **13**, 6.

[B 48] Campion, Sir Harry, 'Recent developments in official economic statistics', *JRSS*, 1958, **121**, 1.

[B 49] Lock G. F. 'Statistics for politicians,' *Statistical News*, 1971, **12**, 9.

[B 50] Mackenzie, W. J. M. and Grove, J. W. *Central Administration in Britain*, Longmans, 1966.

[B 51] Moser, C. A. 'The future role of the Central Statistical Office,' *Statistical News* 1968, **1**, 1.

[B 52] — 'Some general developments in social statistics,' *Social Trends*, 1970, **1**, 7.

[B 53] — 'The statistician in government: a challenge for the 1970s,' *Transactions of the Manchester Statistical Society*, 10 March 1971.

[B 54] Mosley, R. K. *The Story of the Cabinet Office*, Routledge, 1969.

[B 55] Park, A. T. 'Northern Ireland government statistics,' *Statistical News*, 1968, **2**, 12.

[B 56] Pyatt, G. 'British economic statistics,' *JRSS*, 1968, **131**, 35.

[B 57] Rew, R. H. 'Improvement of official statistics,' *JRSS*, 1909, **72**, 731.

[B 58] Willson, F. M. G. *The Organisation of British Central Government 1914–1964*, Allen & Unwin, 2nd ed., 1968.

[B 59] Zinkin, M. and Booer, T. G. 'Statistics for business planning,' *JRSS*, 1968, **131**, 61.

4   OTHER WORKS, WITHOUT NAMED PERSON AS AUTHOR

[B 60] 'Basic United Kingdom statistical sources—where to consult them,' *Board of Trade Journal*, 11 Feb. 1970, pp. 379–83.

[B 61] *British Official Statistics*. Discussion meeting of the Royal Statistical Society, 15 November 1967. *JRSS*, **130**, 1. (Two of the papers at this meeting are cited separately—[B 56] and [B 59].)

[B 62] *British Statistics—a Select List of Sources*. University of Essex Library Reference Leaflet No. 3, 1972.

[B 63] *The Civil Service—Report of the Committee 1966–1968*. Cmnd. 3638.

[B 64] 'Developments in home financial statistics,' CSO, *Economic Trends*, Sep. 1962.

[B 65] 'Developments in official economic statistics, 1957–63', CSO, *Economic Trends*, Feb. 1964. (Reprinted in [B 20].)

[B 66] Economic statistics. Information Division of the Treasury. *Economic Progress Report* Aug., Sep. and Oct. 1970.

[B 67] *Economic Statistics Collections: a Directory of Research Resources in the United Kingdom for Business Industry and Public Affairs*. The Library Association, 1970.

[B 68] *Government Statistical Services*. The Treasury. HMSO, 2nd ed., 1962. [This contains a list of the main subjects on which each government department collects statistics (considerably affected by successive reorganizations) and a list of principal statistical publications, arranged by subject.]

[B 69] *Government Statistical Services—Fourth Report from the Estimates Committee, Session 1966–7*. HC 246 of 1966–7.

[B 70] *Government Statistical Services—Departmental Observations on the Fourth Report from the Estimates Committee, Ninth Special Report from the Committee, Session 1966–7*. HC 444 of 1966–7.

[B 71] *House of Commons Debates*, 17 April 1956, cols. 867–9.

[B 72] *House of Commons Debates*, 1 Aug. 1956, cols. 1400–4.

[B 73] *House of Commons Debates*, 5 Feb. 1963, cols. 406–16. Adjournment debate on *Social Changes in Britain*, produced by the COI but not made generally available.

[B 74] *House of Commons Debates*, 26 April 1966, written answers, col. 17.

[B 75] *House of Commons Debates*, 4 May 1967, cols. 754–854. Debate on item [B 69].

[B 76] *House of Commons Debates*, 23 Oct. 1967, written answers, col. 388.

[B 77] *The Housing Programme 1965 to 1970*. Ministry of Housing and Local Government, 1965, Cmnd. 2838. Appendix 3—improvement in sources of information.

[B 78] *Information and the Public Interest*. Presented by the Prime Minister, Cmnd. 4089, 1969.

[B 79] 'Memorandum on official statistics,' Council of the Royal Statistical Society, *JRSS*, 1943, **106**, 145.

[B 80] *National Board for Prices and Incomes—Report No. 170, Supplement*. Fifth and Final General Report July 1969 to March 1971, Supplement. 1971, Cmnd. 4649—I.

[B 81] *Official Publications*. Treasury, 1958. (Reprinted 1963.)

[B 82] *Official Statistics Committee, Second and Third Reports.* HC 39 of 1881.

[B 83] 'Recent developments in official economic statistics,' CSO, *Economic Trends*, May 1957.

[B 84] *Recommended Basic Statistical Sources for Community Use.* The Library Association, 2nd ed., 1970. (Earlier ed. also in *JRSS*, 1969, **132**, 122.)

[B 85] *Recruitment to the Civil Service—Sixth Report from the Estimates Committee, Session 1964–5.* HC 308 of 1964–5.

[B 86] *Report of the Committee on the Provision for Economic and Social Research*, Cmd. 6868, 1946.

[B 87] *Reports of the Council on Prices, Productivity and Incomes.* First, 1958; Second, 1958; Third, 1959; Fourth, 1961. All HMSO.

[B 88] *Reports of the Interdepartmental Committee on Social and Economic Research*—October 1948, Cmd. 7537; December 1950, Cmd. 8091; May 1956, HMSO.

[B 89] *Report on the Collection and Presentation of Official Statistics.* Treasury, HMSO, 1921.

[B 90] *Second Report of the Joint Committee on the Publication of Proceedings in Parliament*, HL 109, HC 261 of 1969–70.

[B 91] 'Seminar on business statistics and information for the manufacturing and construction industries,' *Journal and Proceedings of the Industrial Marketing Association*, Vol. 6, No. 1, Feb. 1970.

[B 92] *Social Science Research Council, Annual Report 1970–1*, HC 529 of 1970–1.

[B 93] *Standard Industrial Classification.* CSO. First published 1948. 3rd ed., HMSO, 1968.

[B 94] *Standard Industrial Classification, Alphabetical List of Industries.* CSO. First published 1959. 2nd ed., HMSO, 1968. Amendments were published in 1969.

[B 95] Statistics users conferences. Notes in *Statistical News*, Feb. 1971, p. 12.31; Aug. 1971, p. 16.34; Aug. 1972, p. 18.35; May 1973, p. 21.33; May 1974, p. 25.30

[B 96] Statistics users conference. *Social Science Research Council Newsletter No. 11*, March 1971, p. 20.

[B 97] 'Survey of collections of economic statistics in the United Kingdom—note by the Committee of Librarians and Statisticians,' *Statistical News*, 1972, **18**, 21.

[B 98] 'Survey of holdings of basic statistical source material in United Kingdom libraries,' *Library Association Record*, May 1970, pp. 208–9.

[B 99] *Union List of Statistical Serials in British Libraries.* The Library Association, 1972.

5(a) SUPPLEMENT OF ADDITIONAL REFERENCES—LATE ENTRIES

[B 100] *Background Briefing Number 6—Statistics.* Department of Employment, 1972. Available from Information Branch, Department of Employment.

[B 101] *Government Statistics—a Brief Guide to Sources.* CSO, 1973, free. To be updated from time to time. Contains a list of the main government statistical publications, and of departmental responsibilities and contact points. Available from CSO, CO:CSO Section.

[B 102] Allen, R. G. D. 'Official Economic Statistics,' *Economica*, 1956, XXIII (N.S.), 360.

[B 103] Fessey, M. C. 'Some developments in economic statistics since 1934,' *The Statistician*, 1969, **19**, 105.

[B 104] Stavely, R. (ed.) *Government Information and the Research Worker*, The Library Association, 1st ed., 1952. Chapter X by D. E. Locke on the Central Statistical Office.

[B 105] Stavely, R. and Piggott, M. (eds.) *Government Information and the Research Worker*, The Library Association, 2nd ed., 1965. Chapter X by L. M. Feery on the Interdepartmental Committee on Social and Economic Research.

[B 106] *Research and Development—First Report from the Select Committee on Science and Technology, Session 1971–2.* HC 237 of 1971–2.

[B 107] Royal Commission on the Constitution 1969–73. Vol. II. *Memorandum of Dissent* by Lord Crowther-Hunt and Professor A. T. Peacock. Cmnd. 5460–1.

[B 108] 'Statistics for government', PEP. *Planning*, 1957, XXIII, No. 406.

[B 109] *Tax-Credit—Evidence taken by the Select Committee on Tax Credit, Session 1972–3*, HC 341-II of 1972–3.

[B 110] Rokkan, S. and Meyriat, J. (eds.) *International Guide to Electoral Statistics, Vol. 1: National Elections in Western Europe*, Mouton, The Hague and Paris, 1969. Chapter on the UK by D. Butler and J. Cornford.

[B 111] Craig, F. W. S. *British Parliamentary Election Statistics 1918–1970*, Political Reference Publications, Chichester 1971. There is a good bibliography on election statistics.

[B 112] Carr-Saunders, A. M. and Jones, D. C. *A Survey of the Social Structure of England and Wales, as illustrated by statistics*, OUP, 2nd ed,. 1937.

[B 113] Edwards, B. *Sources of Social Statistics*, Heinemann, 1974.

[B 114] Hamilton, G. E. and Smart, K. I. *United Kingdom Statistics: Sources, Use and Indexing Requirements*, Loughborough University of Technology Library, 1974.

[B 115] *A Guide to Health and Social Service Statistics.* DHSS, 1974.

[B 116] *Report of the Committee on Social Studies*, Cmnd. 2660, 1965.

5(b) SUPPLEMENT OF ADDITIONAL REFERENCES

Statistical series mentioned as examples in the text. All items in this sub-section are published by HMSO as non-parliamentary papers, unless otherwise stated. Items [B 117] to [B 130] are discontinued series, in alphabetical order of title. Items [B 131] to [B 172] are current series or individual publications, also in alphabetical order of title.

[B 117] *Abstract of Labour Statistics*, Command Papers. Occasional, latterly triennial. To 1937.

[B 118] *Annual Report of the Ministry of Labour*, Command Papers. To 1960.

[B 119] *Annual Report on Colonial Territories*, Command Papers. To 1961–2.

[B 120] *Civil Aviation Business Monitors.* Various series—annual, quarterly, and monthly. To 1972.

[B 121] *Digest of Colonial Statistics.* Annual, formerly quarterly. To August 1966.

[B 122] *Digest of Statistics analysing Certificates of Incapacity for Work.* Annual. DHSS. To 1969–70.

[B 123] *Housing Statistics.* Quarterly. To Feb. 1972.

[B 124] *Overseas Economic Surveys.* A series of separate publications on selected countries. To 1959.

[B 125] *Protective Duties.* Annual. To 1965.

[B 125A] *Public Investment in Great Britain.* Command Papers. Annual 1960–3.

[B 126] *Report on Overseas Trade.* Monthly. To Feb. 1971.

[B 127] *Road Motor Vehicles.* Annual. To 1962.

[B 128] *Statistical Abstract for the British Commonwealth and the Sterling Area.* Annual. To 1967.

[B 129] *Statistical Summary, Bank of England.* Monthly. Bank of England. To Dec. 1945.

[B 130] *Times Review of Industry and Technology.* Monthly. Times Newspapers. To Oct. 1967.

[B 131] *Account of the British Aid Programme. Text of United Kingdom Memorandum to the Development Assistance Committee of the OECD.* Annual. Command Paper in 1973, formerly non-parliamentary.

[B 132] *Annual Report of the Department of Education and Science.* Recently non-parliamentary, formerly Command Papers.

[B 133] *Annual Report of the Scottish Development Department.* Command Papers.

[B 134] *Britain in Brief.* Annual.

[B 135] *Bulletin of Labour Statistics.* Quarterly. International Labour Office, Geneva.

[B 136] *Canada Yearbook.* Annual. Information Canada, Ottawa.

[B 137] *CEGB Statistical Yearbook.* Annual. Central Electricity Generating Board.

[B 138] *Census 1961, Great Britain, General Report*, 1968.

[B 139] *Changes in Rates of Wages and Hours of Work.* Monthly.

[B 140] *Civil Service Commission Annual Report.* Civil Service Commission, Basingstoke.

[B 141] *Current Economic Indicators.* Monthly. US Government Printing Office, Washington, DC.

[B 142] *Direction of Trade.* Monthly, plus an annual issue. International Monetary Fund, Washington, DC.

[B 143] *Economic Outlook.* Twice yearly. OECD, Paris.

[B 144] *Education Statistics.* Annual. CIPFA, London.

[B 145] *Facts and Figures about the Church of England Number 3.* Church Information Office, 1965.

[B 146] *Family Expenditure Survey—Handbook on the Sample Fieldwork and Coding Procedures* by W. F. F. Kemsley. 1969.

[B 147] *Financial Statistics—Supplement on Notes and Definitions.* Annual.

[B 148] *Handbook of Statistics (Local Government, Housing and Planning).* Annual. 1965–70.

[B 149] *History of the Second World War.* United Kingdom Civil Series. Edited by Sir Keith Hancock. Twenty-eight Vols. For details see HMSO Sectional List No. 60.

[B 150] *House Condition Survey Report, 1971, England and Wales.* Department of the Environment, 1973.

[B 151] *Housing and Construction Statistics—Notes and Definition Supplement.* Annual.

[B 152] *Housing Survey Reports.* Nos 1–5, HMSO, 1969–70; Nos 6– . Department of the Environment, 1971– .

[B 153] *International Trade.* Annual. General Agreement on Tariffs and Trade, Geneva.

[B 154] *Iron and Steel Industry—Annual Statistics for the United Kingdom.* Annual. Iron and Steel Statistics Bureau, Croydon.

[B 155] *Moodies Investment Handbooks.* 2 vols., quarterly. Moodies Services Ltd.

[B 156] *The Motor Industry of Great Britain.* Annual. SMMT.

[B 157] *New Zealand Official Yearbook.* Annual. Dept. of Statistics, Wellington.

[B 158] *Occasional Bulletin of the Nationwide Building Society.* Irregular. Nationwide Building Society.

[B 159] *Official Yearbook of the Commonwealth of Australia.* Annual. Commonwealth Bureau of Census and Statistics, Canberra.

[B 160] *Progress in Wales—Quarterly Summaries of Economic Developments.* The Welsh Office, Cardiff.

[B 161] *Public Expenditure White Papers—Handbook on Methodology.* 1972.

[B 162] *The Registrar General's Statistical Review for England and Wales—Part III: Commentary.* Annual.

[B 163] *Report on the Census of Distribution and Other Services, 1961. Supplement,* 1972.

[B 164] *Reports on the World Census of Agriculture.* Decennial. Food and Agriculture Organization, Rome.

[B 165] *A Scottish Budget, Estimates of central government revenue and expenditure attributable to Scotland for the financial year 1967–1968.* The Treasury, 1969. Reprinted in the *Minutes of Evidence* of the Select Committee on Scottish Affairs, HC 267–I of 1969–70, pp. 77–88.

[B 166] *Statistical Services of the United States Government.* US Government Printing Office, Washington, DC, 1968.

[B 167] *Statistics for Town and Country Planning.* Irregular. Series I, Planning Decisions, and Series II, Floor Space, HMSO. Series III, Population and Households, Department of the Environment.

[B 168] *Supplementary Statistics relating to Crime.* Annual. The Home Office.

[B 169] *A Survey of German Federal Statistics,* Federal Statistical Office, Wiesbaden. Pub. W. Kohlhammer, Stuttgart, 1971.

[B 170] *Time Rates of Wages and Hours of Work.* Annual.

[B 171] *A Welsh Budget, Estimates of central government revenue and expenditure attributable to Wales for the financial year 1968–1969.* The Treasury, 1971.

[B 172] *Yearbook of Labour Statistics.* Annual. International Labour Office, Geneva.

For further references, see Addenda, p. xvii

TABLE 1: SUBJECT ANALYSIS OF THE CONTENTS OF FIFTEEN GENERAL SOURCES OF STATISTICS

Subject	Abstract of Regional Stats.	Annual Abstract of Statistics	The British Economy: Key Stats. 1900–70	British Labour Stats. Yearbook	Dept. of Employment Gazette	Digest of Stats. for N. Ireland	Digest of Welsh Statistics	Economic Trends	Monthly Digest of Statistics	National Institute Economic Review	Scottish Abstract of Statistics	Scottish Economic Bulletin	Social Trends	Trade and Industry	Ulster Year Book
Area	X	X				X	X				X				X
Climate	X	X					X				X				X
Environment							X						X		
Population and vital stats.	X	X	X			X	X		X		X		X		X
Education	X	X	X			X	X				X		X		X
Other social services	X	X				X	X				X		X		X
Housing	X	X	X			X	X		X		X	X	X		X
Justice and Crime		X				X	X				X		X		
Other social conditions (a)		X				X	X				X		X		
Labour	X	X	X	X	X	X	X	X	X	X	X	X		X	X
Productivity				X	X		X			X		X		X	
Production	X	X	X			X	X	X	X	X	X	X		X	X
Energy	X	X	X			X	X	X	X		X	X		X	X
Construction		X	X			X	X	X	X		X			X	
Agriculture and Food	X	X	X			X	X	X	X		X			X	X
Fisheries		X				X			X					X	
Distribution	X	X	X			X	X	X	X		X	X		X	
Catering	X	X				X			X						
Transport and communications	X	X	X			X	X	X	X	X	X	X	X	X	X
Tourism		X	X			X		X	X	X	X	X		X	X
External trade	X	X	X			X	X	X	X	X	X	X	X	X	X
External finance	X	X	X	X	X (b)	X	X	X	X	X	X	X		X	X
Personal incomes	X	X	X	X	X (b)	X	X	X	X		X	X		X	
Consumers' expenditure		X	X			X		X	X				X	X	
Leisure		X	X			X			X						
Nat. income and expenditure	X	X	X			X	X	X	X	X	X	X	X	X	X
Capital expenditure		X	X			X	X	X	X	X	X	X		X	X
Stocks		X	X			X		X	X	X				X	X
Home finance		X	X			X	X	X	X	X	X			X	
Profits		X	X	X		X		X	X	X	X			X	
Banking, insurance and financial institutions	X	X	X	X	X	X		X	X	X				X	
Prices	X	X	X		X	X	X	X	X	X	X	X	X	X	X

(a) E.g. abortions, adoptions, infectious diseases, liquor licensing, venereal disease.
(b) Not in each monthly issue – articles at intervals on the Family Expenditure Survey.

Subject Index